FINANCIAL INTERMEDIATION BEYOND THE DEBT CRISIS

FINANCIAL INTERMEDIATION BEYOND THE DEBT CRISIS

Donald R. Lessard
John Williamson

INSTITUTE FOR INTERNATIONAL ECONOMICS
WASHINGTON, DC
SEPTEMBER 1985

Dr. Donald R. Lessard, a Visiting Fellow at the Institute during the summer of 1985, is Professor of International Management at the MIT Sloan School of Management and currently Visiting Professor of International Management at Stanford University's Graduate School of Business. Dr. Lessard has published extensively on various aspects of international finance including corporate finance, portfolio investment, and external financing for developing countries.

Dr. John Williamson is a Senior Fellow at the Institute for International Economics. He was formerly economics professor at the Pontifícia Universidade Católica do Rio de Janeiro, University of Warwick, Massachusetts Institute of Technology, and taught at the University of York and Princeton University; Advisor to the International Monetary Fund; and Economic Consultant to Her Majesty's Treasury.

ACKNOWLEDGEMENTS

The authors acknowledge with gratitude interviews willingly granted them by a number of officials of financial institutions; the helpful comments of participants in seminars held in Bogotá, Hawaii, London, New York, and Washington; and the many suggestions of colleagues and referees.   D.R.L. and J.W.

INSTITUTE FOR INTERNATIONAL ECONOMICS

C. Fred Bergsten, *Director*
Kathleen A. Lynch, *Director of Publications*

The Institute for International Economics was created, and is principally funded, by the German Marshall Fund of the United States.

The views expressed in this publication are those of the authors. This publication is part of the overall program of the Institute, as endorsed by its Board of Directors, but does not necessarily reflect the views of individual members of the Board or the Advisory Committee.

Library of Congress Cataloging-in-Publication Data
Lessard, Donald R.
Financial intermediation beyond the debt crisis.
"September 1985."
Bibliography: p. 115
1. Loans, Foreign. 2. International finance.
I. Williamson, John, 1937– . II. Institute for
International Economics (U.S.) III. Title.
HG3891.5.L47 1985 336.3'435'091724 85–18092
ISBN 0–88132–021–8

*Dedicated to the memory of Carlos Diaz-Alejandro
1937–1985*

*whose untimely death deprived the Institute of one of
the most respected and valuable members of its
Advisory Committee, and whose interest and research
helped stimulate this study.*

Preface

The problem of international debt has been one of the major research topics at the Institute during the past three years. We have published two comprehensive studies on the subject by William R. Cline, *International Debt and the Stability of the World Economy* (September 1983) and *International Debt: Systemic Risk and Policy Response* (September 1984). Two publications by John Williamson have focused on the role of the International Monetary Fund: *The Lending Policies of the International Monetary Fund* (August 1982) and *IMF Conditionality* (May 1983). We have held two conferences on key aspects of the debt problem and countries heavily involved in it, both leading to special reports edited by John Williamson: *Prospects for Adjustment in Argentina, Brazil, and Mexico* (June 1983) and *Inflation and Indexation: Argentina, Brazil, and Israel* (March 1985). Our most recent study on the topic analyzed *Bank Lending to Developing Countries: The Policy Alternatives* (April 1985 by C. Fred Bergsten, William R. Cline, and John Williamson).

The present study looks beyond the crisis stage of the debt problem to the ongoing needs of the developing countries for external finance. It asks both how the desired quantity of funds can be attracted, and how the quality of those flows can be improved inter alia to avoid recreating the problem that has emerged from excessive reliance on short-term bank credits. To these ends, the authors explore a wide range of innovations in both the private financial markets and the role of the public international institutions—and recommend a series of specific steps to promote effective financial intermediation beyond the debt crisis.

In carrying out their research, as with most projects at the Institute, the authors were assisted by several meetings attended by knowledgeable observers of the issue. In light of the need to tap expertise from both creditor and debtor countries, private markets, and official quarters, meetings on this study were held in Europe, Hawaii (with Japanese experts), and Latin America as well as in New York and Washington. We particularly wish to thank our local hosts for three of these sessions: The Foundation for Higher Education and Development (FEDESARROLLO) in Bogotá, Goldman Sachs in New York, and S.G. Warburg and Co., Ltd., in London. The final draft of the study was rigorously reviewed by a number of experts outside the Institute, whose views were carefully considered in preparation of the final manuscript.

The Institute for International Economics is a private, nonprofit research institution for the study and discussion of international economic issues. Its purpose is to analyze important topics in this area of public policy, and to develop and communicate practical new approaches for dealing with them. The Institute is completely nonpartisan.

The Institute was created in November 1981 through a generous funding commitment from the German Marshall Fund of the United States. Substantial support is now also being provided by a number of other private foundations and corporations. This particular study was partially funded by the Tinker Foundation and the United States–Japan Foundation, whose support is deeply appreciated.

The Board of Directors bears overall responsibility for the Institute and gives general guidance and approval to its research program—including identification of topics that are likely to become important to international economic policymakers over the medium run (generally, one to three years) and which thus should be addressed by the Institute. The Director of the Institute, working closely with the staff and outside Advisory Committee, is responsible for the development of particular projects and makes the final decision to publish an individual study.

The Institute hopes that its studies and other activities will contribute to building a stronger foundation for international economic policy around the world. Comments as to how it can best do so are invited from readers of these publications.

C. FRED BERGSTEN
Director
September 1985

viii

Contents

TEXT FIGURES

Glossary

AICPA	American Institute of Certified Public Accountants
BIS	Bank for International Settlements
ECU	European currency unit
ERISA	Employee Retirement and Income Security Act
FRN	Floating rate note
IDA	International Development Association
IDB	Inter-American Development Bank
IFC	International Finance Corporation
IMF	International Monetary Fund
LIBOR	London Inter-Bank Offer Rate
MDB	Multilateral development bank
MIGA	Multilateral Investment Guarantee Authority
NIF	Note issuance facility
ODA	Official development assistance
OECD	Organization for Economic Cooperation and Development
OPEC	Organization of Petroleum Exporting Countries
OPIC	Overseas Private Investment Corporation
REIT	Real estate investment trust
RIAC	Reimbursable interest-averaging cap
RUF	Revolving underwriting facility
SDR	Special drawing right
TLI	Transferable loan instrument
WPI	Wholesale price index

1 Introduction

This study is concerned with the magnitude and form of the external borrowing of developing countries in the coming years. It is vital that this topic receive serious thought today, even before the bulk of the debtor countries regain normal access to capital markets, if international capital mobility is to realize its potential in the future.

Our analysis indicates that on present trends, even under relatively optimistic assumptions regarding the world economy, the flow of external finance to developing countries is likely to remain substantially less than would be desirable. We also see little reason to expect a major shift away from the past dominance of general obligation, floating-rate credits, despite their increasingly evident shortcomings.

It would be unrealistic to expect that this unsatisfactory state of affairs can be remedied overnight. But neither is it immutable: attitudes can change and actions can be conceived that would both stimulate the volume of flows in the short run and change their structure in the longer run. The aims of the study are to develop suggestions for the instruments that could be used to those ends and the actions that would be needed to change present prospects for the better.

In what we now think of as the golden age of international lending prior to World War I, capital flowed from the capital-abundant industrial countries to the capital-hungry "areas of recent settlement," like Canada, Australia, Argentina, and, in the nineteenth century, the United States. Despite periodic defaults, most participants benefited from this flow—the borrowers from accelerated development, the lenders from higher returns than were available at home (Fishlow 1985; World Bank 1985, pp. 12–15). A major reason was that lending took a form—predominantly long-term, fixed-interest bonds— that was reasonably suited to the needs of both borrowers and lenders under the circumstances of low inflation then prevailing.

In contrast, a series of disasters has marked international lending since 1914. The borrowing of Europe and Latin America in the 1920s ended with

1

defaults far more widespread than had been experienced in the nineteenth century. Hot money flows from Europe in the 1930s severely disrupted economic policy. The recycling of the oil surplus in the 1970s led to the debt crisis of the 1980s. Now a flood of money is financing an excessive budget deficit in the world's most capital-rich country, posing a serious threat of a new world economic crisis in the next few years (Marris, forthcoming 1985).

The *potential* benefits of international capital flows are beyond doubt. They can shift savings from areas of low to areas of high productivity—as they did prior to 1914, and as they have done since in specific cases, notably where they permitted the exploitation of natural resources (like oil) which could not have been developed with domestic capital alone. They can also shift foreign exchange to areas where this is temporarily in unusually short supply and therefore of temporarily high value in maintaining output—a situation of immediate relevance to many debtor countries (section 2). Further, they can shift risks associated with particular development strategies or economic ventures to investors with comparative advantage in bearing them, for example because of greater scope for diversification. But, to realize all these possibilities, it will be necessary to shift the structure of international lending as well as to restore an adequate and stable volume of flows.

At the moment most debtor countries do not have much choice as to how much or in what form they borrow, but that will become progressively less true as they recover from the debt crisis. Projections undertaken by William R. Cline (1984) at the Institute for International Economics suggest that a number of the major debtors should be on the threshold of restoring their creditworthiness by around 1987, provided that two sets of conditions are satisfied. One is that the members of the Organization for Economic Cooperation and Development (OECD) maintain relatively open markets and a reasonable macroeconomic performance—i.e., that they avoid a new recession and a renewed interest-rate spiral, and that there be some correction of the overvaluation of the dollar (in which most debt is denominated). The other is that the debtor countries continue to pursue the adjustment efforts on which they have embarked, and are spared the advent of populist governments bent on confrontation rather than self-interest.

These conditions cannot be taken for granted. (Moreover, some economists have argued that Cline's projections are overly optimistic: see, for example, Dornbusch and Fischer 1984, Fishlow 1984.) Nevertheless, the prospect of progress in resolving the debt crisis is now sufficiently real to justify turning attention to what needs to be done as countries restore normal, voluntary access to the international capital market. Indeed, there may well be scope for restructuring the form of debt in multiyear reschedulings in ways that would help prepare the way for a return to normal market access. This adds to the urgency of developing a clear vision of the direction in which the system should move over the coming years.

Restoration of voluntary market access is unlikely to involve a return to the situation of the 1970s, where borrowing was limited only by demand. It is much more probable that the current position of Turkey or India will become typical. Turkey undertook its major rescheduling and adjustment program in 1980, and in 1984 began to be able once again to borrow limited sums from the banks without a concerted package deal. India has followed prudent policies for a long time (including borrowing from the International Monetary Fund, IMF, in preference to the commercial banks in 1981), and is now considered creditworthy by the bond market as well as the banks—although no one imagines that would remain true for long if India started to borrow massively.

The prospective adequacy of capital flows to developing countries in the next few years is examined in section 2. It is concluded that there would be benefits from a flow significantly greater than is in prospect from traditional sources over the next few years, given the scale of the cutback in commercial bank lending, which seems unlikely to be reversed. Thus, a desire to increase the volume of external finance provides one strong reason for asking whether alternative sources might be tapped.

A complementary reason for such an enquiry is that capital mobility can be expected to yield its potential benefits only if the structure of lending matches the needs of both borrowers and lenders. The flows of bank credit that dominated the 1970s did not match the needs of the borrowers. The invention of the rollover loan with a floating interest rate seemed at the time to be a marvelous development from the standpoint of the lenders, but it turned out that the resulting concentration of risk on the borrowers was more than they could absorb. When the world economy imposed a series of adverse shocks on them in the early 1980s, the borrowers had no option but to seek extensive rescheduling—thus pushing some of the risk back to the lenders after all, at the same time imposing very heavy costs on the borrowers in the form of a decade's interruption in growth. In comparison, the added growth achieved by borrowing in the 1970s was modest, for the foreign-exchange constraint was at that time far less binding than it became in the early 1980s.

Section 3 of the study analyzes the principles on which international finance needs to be restructured to achieve a more efficient international distribution of risk and a more appropriate distribution over time of debt-service obligations. The objective is to permit exploitation of comparative advantage in risk bearing through financial transactions, just as the international trading system permits the exploitation of comparative advantage in production capabilities through trade. Both borrowers and lenders would gain from such a system.

Most nonconcessional financing secured by developing countries has in the past taken one of two forms: either *direct investment,* in which the investor maintains control of the investment and is rewarded by the profits, or *general obligation borrowing,* in which the borrower undertakes to use his general revenues to service his debt on terms independent of the success of the investment made with the loan. Both forms of financing have a legitimate role—the former where the investor contributes intangible assets (like technology or know-how) that he wishes to retain under his control, and the latter where the lender has little or no capacity to assess or share in the risks of investment.

In addition to those extreme cases, however, there are many instances in which a foreign investor may not seek or desire control, but would be well-suited and willing to bear some of the risk involved in investment, in return for a commensurate gain if the investment prospers. The debt crisis has shown how much borrowers, too, have at stake in spreading some of their risks. Faint signs of a trend toward investment instruments that involve higher expected returns associated with risk sharing but without control can already be detected: for example, the expanding role of the International Finance Corporation (IFC); minority participation in joint ventures, production-sharing contracts, and other "new forms" of international investment (Oman 1984); and a trickle of portfolio investment in equities quoted on the "emerging markets" of some developing countries.

A principal objective of section 4 is to examine how this desirable trend might be reinforced and amplified. The primary focus is on examining instruments that might achieve a better structure of international lending in the longer term, but in the hope that this might also help to increase capital flows in the shorter run. Tackling the problem in this way should avoid the danger of prolonging or rekindling the debt crisis as a result of any success in increasing capital flows.

Merely recognizing that the prospective volume of external finance is inadequate and that its existing structure is flawed, though, will not result in the required changes. Bank debt came to dominate the external financing of the developing countries for many reasons, including the borrowers' desire to minimize foreign involvement in the management of their economies and the banks' need to find new borrowers, and was not discouraged by the IMF or the World Bank. The banks will not easily be replaced by other lenders. Concerted action by borrowers, lenders, and the multilateral institutions will be required to increase the volume and change the structure of external finance. The final section of this study contains proposals for action to achieve those ends.

2   The Volume of External Finance

This section deals with the volume of external finance that the developing countries are likely to need and to be able to command in the medium term. It starts by presenting recent projections of the likely size of developing country current account deficits in 1987—a natural year on which to focus attention, given the hope that by then the bulk of the debtor countries will no longer need the crutch of concerted, involuntary lending. This is followed by an attempt to project likely sources, and competing uses, of external finance. The section concludes with an assessment of the adequacy of the projected flows.

Projected Current Account Deficits

Projecting the current account deficits of developing countries was a popular activity in 1984, although interest seems to have flagged in 1985. Table 1 shows a number of these projections. Unfortunately, it is difficult to compare them because of their different country coverage, coupled with the fact that some studies do not present figures for individual countries.

Perhaps surprisingly, a second potential difficulty in comparing projections is not a major problem: the *assumptions* that underlie these projections are

TABLE 1   Current account balance projections, 1986–87 (billion dollars)

Country group	Actual current account balance 1981	1983	Source of projection	Projected current account balance 1986	1987
Brazil, Chile,	− 30.4	− 2.5	Cline	− 5.0	− 0.4
and Mexico			Enders/Mattione	n.a.	− 7.7
			Morgan Guaranty	− 3.5	n.a.
			IDB-A	− 1.0	1.1
			IDB-B	− 12.3	− 13.2
6 major Latin	− 32.7	0.0	Cline	− 8.0	− 8.2
debtors			Enders/Mattione	n.a.	− 7.7
			IDB-A	− 6.8	− 5.7
			IDB-B	− 20.5	− 23.8
7 major borrowers	− 35.7	− 10.9	IMF	− 3.0	− 3.5
12 major oil	− 39.1	− 24.0[a]	Cline	− 20.0	− 13.6
importers			Fishlow	− 28.6	n.a.
19 major debtors	− 54.2	− 22.7	Cline	− 42.9	− 38.0
Nonoil developing countries	− 108.3	− 52.1	IMF	− 35.4	− 44.5
Indebted developing countries	− 112.6	− 59.4	IMF	− 36.7	− 46.1

n.a. Not available.

Source: Cline, *International Debt*, tables 8.2–8.4; Enders and Mattione, *Latin America: The Crisis of Debt and Growth*, table 9, and figures supplied by authors; Morgan Guaranty, *World Financial Markets*, Oct./Nov. 1984, table 10; Fishlow, "The Debt Crisis: Round Two Ahead?", table 3; IMF, *World Economic Outlook*, April 1985, appendix tables 36 and 51, and Fund staff for 1987 estimates; Inter-American Development Bank, *External Debt and Economic Development in Latin America: Background and Prospects*, Tables A.1.04–A.1.10.

a. Fishlow (who used less recent data) gives the 1983 current deficit as 30.9 billion.

broadly similar. As can be seen from table 2, all of the projections postulate continuing, though moderate, OECD growth, interest rates with the London Inter-Bank Offer Rate (LIBOR) in the region of 10 percent, continuing moderate inflation in the industrial countries, and no major change in the oil price. Views differ most significantly on two topics that not all forecasters seem to consider relevant: the outlook for the dollar exchange rate and for commodity prices. Finally, all the projections foresee some resumption of growth in the debtor countries, though not to the rates prevailing prior to the debt crisis.

TABLE 2   **Principal assumptions underlying current balance projections[a]**

	Cline	Enders/ Mattione	Morgan Guaranty	IDB	IMF[b]
OECD growth (annual percentage)	2.7	c.3	2.4	2.5	3.1
LIBOR (percentage)	10.3	10.9	10	c.10	9.0
Dollar depreciation (annual percentage)	6.7	n.a.	3.5	n.a.	0.1
OECD inflation (annual percentage)	6	n.a.	6	7	3.8
Oil price (dollars per barrel)	33	35	27	33	28
Commodity prices (annual percentage change)	endogenous	2.4	6.5	n.a.	n.a.

				Scenario A	Scenario B	
Debtor country growth (annual percentage)						
Aggregate	n.a.	n.a.	n.a.	2.7	5.4	4.5
Brazil	4.5	−1.2	5.0	2.7	5.4	n.a.
Chile	4.5	5.5	2.0	2.7	5.4	n.a.
Mexico	4.5	1.6	4.2	2.7	5.4	n.a.
Korea	7.5	n.a.	n.a.	n.a.	n.a.	n.a.
Others	4.5	c.3.7	n.a.	2.7	5.4	n.a.

n.a. No assumption specified.
Note: Fishlow accepts Cline's assumptions except for certain behavioral relationships.
Source: Supporting material to tables cited for table 1.
a. Average of 1985–86 and, where applicable, 1987.
b. Assumes that 1987–90 average applies to 1987.

Table 1 shows various projections for 1986 and 1987, as well as actual current account outcomes for similar groups of countries in 1981 and 1983. Two conclusions are suggested by these data. First, a very substantial adjustment was accomplished between 1981, the year of the peak deficit, and 1983. The aggregate current account deficit declined by some $50 billion, about 50 percent, of which about half was accounted for by the limited group of major debtors. Further progress in reducing the deficit was recorded in 1984. Second, all the projections except Scenario B of the Inter-American Development Bank (IDB) envisage the deficit remaining at roughly the present level for the next few years, rather than either falling substantially further or returning toward the peak levels of 1979–81. The scenario envisaged is one of moderate export-led growth, in which imports rise (to fuel domestic growth) in pace with exports (which expand as a result of Northern growth and delayed adjustment to the more competitive exchange rates now in effect in most debtor countries).

On the basis of table 1, a base-case estimate of the current account deficit (on goods, services, and private transfers) of all nonoil developing countries in 1987 may be taken as $45 billion.[1] This figure is almost identical in nominal terms to the average deficit in 1977–78 just prior to the second oil price increase, but much smaller in real terms.[2]

This estimate may be considered optimistic by some—especially associated with the assumption of a return to moderate growth (typically around 4 percent to 5 percent a year) in the developing countries. The deficit would undoubtedly be substantially larger if the OECD went into another recession and the developing countries continued growing. In fact, however, such a conjunction would probably be precluded by a lack of finance (see below). The pessimists would expect not so much a bigger current account deficit as slower developing-country growth.

The above projections were based on the outlook for the debtor countries. It may be asked whether they are consistent with expected current account developments of other groups of countries. A forthcoming Institute study by Stephen Marris (1985) offers projections of the US balance of payments under various hypotheses about, in particular, the future course of the dollar's exchange rate. Under his base case, in which the dollar remains at the average level it reached in October 1984–March 1985, the US current account deficit is projected at some $200 billion in 1987. Under his alternative

---

1. The IDB model assumes that export growth and import substitution are exogenous with respect to the real exchange rate of the debtor countries. Although the projections made some allowance for the import substitution already achieved, the model's exclusion of the possibility of further expenditure switching precludes any possibility of success for the strategy of export-led growth now being pursued. (Expenditure switching is defined as a change in the proportion of expenditure—whether foreign or domestic—directed to home-produced at the expense of foreign-produced goods. Such a redirection of expenditure is typically sought by a change in price incentives, for example, from a real devaluation.) Since we do not regard this as reasonable, the IDB's Scenario B is disregarded in selecting a consensus projection.

2. US prices will have risen about 70 percent in the intervening period, as measured by the GNP deflator.

scenarios, in which the dollar depreciates gradually over a three-year period starting in mid-1985, there is still a very substantial US current deficit in 1987: only with depreciation of over 16 percent a year might the current deficit be less than $100 billion by that year. The disappearance of the Organization of Petroleum Exporting Countries (OPEC) surplus has also provided room for the improvement in the current balance of the nonoil developing countries to be sustained in the future.

Marris argues that US deficits of the size in prospect without a sharp dollar depreciation cannot be financed indefinitely without undermining confidence in the dollar. Nevertheless, the fact that large deficits have developed provides some reassurance against the fear that the developed countries would act to defend their own current account positions and so preclude maintenance of the improved position of the developing countries. One danger will come if the dollar experiences a sharp decline, and the United States is forced into restrictive policies to prevent the reacceleration of inflation. If at that point the other OECD countries accept their responsibility to expand demand and allow a deterioration in their current balances, the threat to the overall position of the developing countries will be limited: the main impact would be on the *direction* rather than the *level* of their trade. If, however, the other OECD countries remain defensively preoccupied with reducing their fiscal deficits or maintaining net exports, a new recession will be inevitable, and the trade balances of the developing countries would be bound to deteriorate significantly unless they also accepted a new recession.

Another danger will arise if the dollar remains strongly overvalued and provokes a major outbreak of protection, disrupting the world trading system and thereby the prospect of export-led growth in the developing countries. These are the most serious threats to a satisfactory resolution of the debt crisis. In either event the adjustment process would be aided by an expansion of capital flows to developing countries.

Sources and Competing Uses of External Finance

Figure 1 provides an overview of the composition of net capital flows to developing countries from 1960 to 1983. It shows the declining relative importance of official development assistance (ODA) and export credits, and the growth of commercial bank lending.

Table 3 shows more detailed estimates of the external financial flows to

FIGURE 1   **Composition of net capital flows to developing countries, 1960, 1970, 1980, 1983, and projections for 1987**

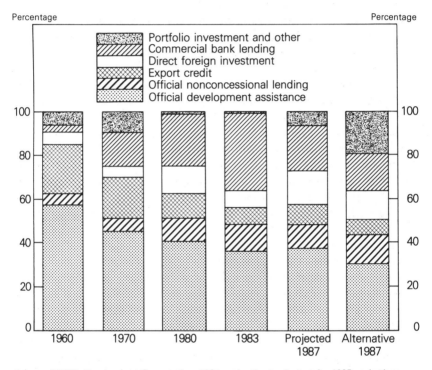

Source: OECD, *Development Co-operation,* 1984, and estimates in text for 1987 projections.

indebted developing countries since 1977.[3] The purpose of assembling these data is to provide a background for assessment of the outlook for the various sources of external finance in the year 1987.

3. This table has been constructed from two data sources which, in the words of the footnote to the IMF table that constituted one of them, "are not always easily reconcilable." In two parts of the table, data from the World Bank's Debtor Reporting System have been employed to provide a disaggregation of the IMF data which is important to the purpose at hand. One of these is to break down official loans into bilateral loans, multilateral loans, and export credits. The totals of the IMF and Bank data were very similar in earlier years, but since 1981 the Fund total has been substantially larger, leaving a big unallocated residual.

The World Bank's data were also employed in distinguishing the sources of private finance.

OFFICIAL TRANSFERS

"Official transfers" comprise that part of official development assistance (or "aid") for which the donor does not expect repayment, even on concessional terms. These transfers were still growing in real terms in the 1970s, but since 1981 the total has stagnated in dollar terms. Projecting stagnation forward to 1987 may, however, prove unduly pessimistic. The Reagan administration, while remaining unsympathetic to multilateral aid, seems willing to contemplate selective increases in bilateral aid as an instrument of foreign policy. In most other OECD donor countries, except the United Kingdom, there is still a trend toward modest increases in aid in terms of national currency, although this has not shown up in increased dollar flows since 1980 due to the appreciation of the dollar. Accordingly, it will be assumed that official transfers will grow in line with inflation, to reach a total of $16 billion in 1987 (table 4).

BILATERAL LOANS

Because bilateral loans are given on concessional terms, they are also included in the definition of aid. Their total has been declining since 1980. The same factors mentioned as reasons for anticipating an end to the real erosion of official transfers, especially a reversal of the dollar's appreciation, may also arrest the decline in bilateral loans. The large unallocated residual in table 3 in 1982–83 also suggests that the decline may be exaggerated by the World Bank data. Bilateral loans in 1987 are therefore projected at $6 billion.

The Bank's figures were adopted for bonds, for other private sources (on which Bank data are poor, though the item is small), and for suppliers' credits.

Bank loans were then calculated as a residual from the IMF's total for private finance (line 8). Total bank loans were broken down by maturity by adopting the Fund's figure for short-term private borrowing, which is reported to consist largely though not exclusively of bank loans. The estimate of concerted lending, or involuntary "new lending," was supplied by the Institute of International Finance.

These procedures are far from perfect, as can be appreciated by comparing the estimates they yield of medium-term bank lending (shown in line 11) with estimates yielded by the World Bank data of $16.7 billion, $23.1 billion, $32.7 billion, $24.4 billion, $29.4 billion, and $33.2 billion for 1977 through 1982. (The Bank's 1983 figure is not comparable since, unlike the Fund, the Bank did not classify the medium-term rescheduling of short-term debt as new medium-term lending.) This seems, however, to be about as good a picture of past sources of external finance as it is possible to construct on the basis of publicly available data.

TABLE 3   **Composition of the net flow of external finance to indebted developing countries, 1977–84 (billion dollars)**

		1977	1978	1979	1980
1	Official finance	22.1	24.5	29.8	36.6
2	Transfers	8.3	8.3	11.7	12.5
3	Bilateral loans	5.8	7.0	7.8	8.3
4	Multilateral loans	5.7	6.5	7.1	9.3
5	Export credits	2.3	2.8	3.9	5.4
6	Unallocated	0	−0.1	−0.7	1.1
7	Direct investment	6.0	7.9	10.1	9.4
8	Private loans	28.2	44.8	52.4	69.7
9	Suppliers' credits	2.3	3.3	4.0	1.8
10	Bank loans	23.7	38.6	47.7	66.8
11	Medium-term	9.0	28.8	38.1	36.4
12	Concerted	—	—	—	—
13	Short-term	14.7	9.8	9.6	30.4
14	Bonds	2.8	3.2	0.9	1.5
15	Other	−0.6	−0.3	−0.2	−0.4
16	Reserves and miscellaneous	−19.4	−20.4	−30.5	−38.6
17	Change in reserves (increase = −)	−10.7	−13.5	−21.5	−18.4
18	SDR allocations, etc.[a]	0.6	1.4	2.9	2.5
19	Reserve creation[b]	2.0	1.4	−1.3	1.9
20	Export credit extended by developing countries, etc.[c]	−6.2	−4.9	−7.8	−7.8
21	Borrowing from IMF	−0.2	−0.4	0.2	1.5
22	Change in arrears (increase = +)	1.6	0.5	0.4	0.8
23	Errors and omissions	−6.5	−4.9	−3.4	−19.1
24	Current account deficit on goods, services, and private transfers	36.9	56.8	61.7	77.0

— Negligible.
n.a. Not available.
Source: IMF, *World Economic Outlook,* appendix table 38, for lines 2, 7, 8, 13, and 17–24, and the sum of lines 3–6. World Bank's Debtor Reporting System for lines 3, 4, 5, 9, 14, and 15. Lines 6, 10, and 11 calculated as residuals. Institute of International Finance for line 12.
a. SDR allocations, valuation adjustments, and gold monetization.
b. Short-term borrowing by monetary authorities from other monetary authorities, excluding the IMF.
c. Described as ''Asset transactions, net'' in *World Economic Outlook.*

MULTILATERAL LOANS

Multilateral loans consist overwhelmingly of lending by the multilateral development banks (MDBs). Part of this lending, notably that through the

1981	1982	1983	1984
40.6	43.4	42.2	42.6
13.5	13.0	12.9	13.1
7.6	5.9	5.0	n.a.
9.6	11.9	10.2	n.a.
5.7	−2.5	5.9	n.a.
4.2	15.1	8.2	n.a.
14.0	12.8	9.9	9.1
84.1	48.1	19.1	13.6
0.6	1.0	1.4	n.a.
82.4	45.9	16.5	n.a.
59.3	32.5	33.8	n.a.
—	1.3	14.6	16.2
23.1	13.4	−17.3	−10.9
1.2	1.3	1.3	n.a.
−0.1	−0.1	−0.1	n.a.
−26.1	−1.3	−11.8	−27.4
1.6	14.4	−9.5	−22.3
0.5	2.9	0.1	0.5
0.9	1.1	−1.3	−0.2
−17.4	−12.9	−8.2	−5.8
6.0	7.0	11.0	5.3
2.0	11.1	7.5	−1.3
−19.7	−24.9	−11.4	−3.6
112.6	102.9	59.4	37.9

International Development Association (IDA), is concessional, but some two-thirds is not. IDA funding has been cut by more than one quarter in nominal terms (and therefore by much more in real terms) in the seventh replenishment that covers 1985–87. The expansion of the flow of nonconcessional finance

TABLE 4   **Projection of the net flow of external finance to indebted developing countries in 1987 (billion dollars)**

	Projected 1987	Actual 1983	Previous peak[a]
Official finance	39	42.2	43.4
Transfers	16	12.9	13.5
Bilateral loans	6	5.0	8.3
Multilateral loans	12	10.2	11.9
Export credits	5	5.9	5.9
Direct investment	11	9.9	14.0
Private loans	20	19.1	84.1
Suppliers' credits	1	1.4	4.0
Bank loans	15	16.5	82.4
Bonds	4	1.3	3.2
Reserves and miscellaneous	−25	−1.8	−38.6
Change in reserves	−11	−9.5	−22.3
SDR allocations, etc.	0	0.1	2.9
Reserve creation	1	−1.3	2.0
Export credit extended by developing countries, etc.	−10	−8.2	−17.4
IMF	−4	11.0	11.0
Change in arrears	−1	7.5	11.1
Errors and omissions	0	−11.4	−24.9
Current account deficit on goods, services, and private transfers	45	59.4	112.6

Source: See text for 1987 projections.
a. Largest absolute number of whatever sign recorded in 1977–84.

from the MDBs has also been checked, but this results from the difficulty of borrowers in mobilizing counterpart funds, a factor that should no longer be operational in 1987. A projection of $12 billion for multilateral loans in 1987 appears reasonable.

EXPORT CREDITS

Official export credits have been high, though erratic, in recent years. This presumably reflects an attempt by developed countries to sustain their exports despite the cutback in commercial bank lending and, in some cases, an intention to temper the effects of the debt crisis. Because the World Bank (1985, box 7.2) believes it may be possible to coax developed countries into increasing export credits, the 1980s average of $4 billion has been increased $1 billion to give $5 billion as the projection for 1987.

DIRECT INVESTMENT

Direct investment occurs when a corporation based in one country (typically a multinational) makes an investment in a company it owns and controls in another country. Such an investment may involve the remittance of funds on an equity basis, retention of profits earned in the host country, the transfer of real resources (notably intangibles like technology), or an intracompany loan. As can be seen from table 3, direct investment in developing countries was expanding rapidly until 1981 but contracted sharply in the ensuing recession and debt crisis.

Outside the extractive industries, the dominant motivation for direct investment has been the desire to gain access to the market of the host country and perhaps that of its neighbors.[4] The collapse of growth prospects in many developing countries since 1981 could therefore have been expected to lead to a fall in direct investment. However, an increasing proportion of direct investment has recently gone into manufacturing for export, a trend that could accelerate with the economic adjustments in response to the debt crisis. A survey of the prospects for direct investment undertaken by the Group of Thirty (1984) in late 1982, shortly after the debt crisis first broke, suggested that the medium-run outlook was for an increase in direct investment.

The Group of Thirty survey gave no hint of the sharp cutback in direct investment recorded in 1983. It did note, however, that multinationals tend to shift working balances around in response to interest differentials and exchange rate fears, and that these shifts influence the figures recorded for direct investment in the balance of payments statistics. Thus, it is reasonable to conclude that a part of the recorded decline may reflect multinational participation in capital flight rather than a cutback in real investment. To that extent the decline is likely to be temporary (or reversed). This assessment is consistent with the fact that the recorded decline in spending of majority-

---

4. See, for example, the response to question 9 in Group of Thirty (1984, p. 30).

owned foreign affiliates of US companies in developing countries was smaller (though still substantial, 22 percent) than that of direct investment shown in table 3, whereas the two series previously moved broadly in parallel. This would suggest that the underlying level of direct investment in 1983 may have been around $10 billion.

The US figures show a near-stabilization of spending in developing countries in 1984, followed by a projected 17 percent increase in 1985 (*Survey of Current Business,* March 1985, p. 24). IMF figures show an 8 percent decline in 1984, with increases in 1985–86 projected to take the total to $11 billion in 1986. That figure would appear a reasonable projection for 1987.

SUPPLIERS' CREDITS

This item includes export credits extended directly by the exporter, as opposed to a governmental export credit agency (included under official finance) or a bank (included under bank loans). It is a small item that tended to decrease during the debt crisis and which seems unlikely to recover much until the debt crisis is securely over. The projection for 1987 will therefore be $1 billion.

BANK LOANS

Loans from commercial banks have since 1977 been the largest and by far the most variable source of external finance. Some trade finance (on short maturities) has always flowed from banks to developing countries, but this was first matched and then surpassed by medium-term syndicated bank credits in the years after the first oil shock. In 1980–81 some countries began to encounter difficulties in borrowing all they desired on medium-term maturities, and turned instead to short-term (nontrade-related) credits.

In the second half of 1982 bank lending collapsed in the "debt crisis." Since then, most new bank lending has taken the form of "concerted" or "involuntary" lending in which the banks collectively agree, along with the IMF and the debtor country, on the minimum amount of finance needed to sustain the agreed adjustment program, and pressure is then brought to bear on individual banks to participate in new lending in proportion to their outstanding exposure. There has also been a major rescheduling of short-term debt, reflected in the large negative entries for short-term bank loans in table 3. (The increase in medium-term loans shown for 1983 and 1984 is in part simply the counter to the reduction in short-term debt.)

Most bankers now appear anxious to reduce their exposure in most developing countries. Even bankers with a strong interest in a continued presence in developing countries suggest that a voluntary resumption of medium-term syndicated lending to more than a handful of the strongest countries is likely to be delayed until at least the turn of the decade. Thus, in 1987 the bulk of new bank lending is likely to be for trade financing, an activity in which many banks have traditionally engaged to oblige their corporate customers. The financing of developing-country export credit is also an expanding business, stimulated by the attractive collateral available. However, to some extent the expansion of trade credit is associated with a rundown of other lending. To trade credit, one must add any remnants of involuntary lending and a minimal level of voluntary syndicated lending to Asia.

Leading bankers have speculated that these factors may support an increase in exposure of perhaps 3 percent in 1987, a flow of some $15 billion. Since bank capital is expected to continue growing substantially faster than this, relative exposure will continue to decline. The figure of $15 billion has been inserted as the estimate in table 4.

BONDS

The volume of bonds issued by developing countries on the capital markets of developed countries (including the international or Eurobond market) fell off in the late 1970s, displaced by the easy availability of bank credit and deterred by the shrinkage of fixed-rate lending in the face of uncertainty regarding inflation and interest rates. However, there are now signs of recovery, as the bond market has moved into an expansionary phase following the widespread adoption of floating rate notes. Countries now perceived as creditworthy by the market include Korea, Malaysia, Papua New Guinea, Singapore, Thailand—and interestingly, India. Indonesia and Mexico are reportedly near the borderline, the former currently just above and the latter just below. A projection for bond finance of $4 billion in 1987, somewhat above the previous peak, does not seem unrealistic. In part this simply reflects a change in the form of bank finance, as individual banks seek to safeguard themselves against rescheduling by replacing syndicated credits by floating rate notes.

RESERVE CHANGES

The value of recorded nongold reserves of the indebted developing countries at the end of March 1985 was some $95 billion (*International Financial Statistics*). Demand for reserves typically grows slightly less rapidly than trade, at perhaps 90 percent of the growth in the value of developing-country imports, which Cline (1984, p. 163) projects at 11 percent in 1987. This suggests that the developing countries will want to add some $11 billion to their reserves in that year. This is similar to the IMF's projection of $11.0 billion reserve growth for these countries in 1986 (IMF 1985, table 38).

SDR ALLOCATIONS, ETC.

This item comprises allocations of special drawing rights (SDRs), valuation adjustments, and gold monetization. The last item is usually small but positive. Since there is no particular reason to expect valuation adjustments to be positive rather than negative, they can be projected at zero. According to the vision prevalent when the SDR scheme was adopted in the late 1960s, SDR allocations should normally have sufficed to satisfy a substantial part of the increase in the demand to hold reserves. This vision is not, however, shared by most of the present members of the Group of Ten (1985, chapter 4); indeed, it is difficult to resist the impression that the US Treasury regards the demand for increased holdings of liquid reserves as a useful source of financing for a part of its own budget deficit. Since the outlook for new SDR allocations appears so bleak, this item is unlikely to reach $1 billion and is therefore projected at zero.

RESERVE CREATION

To a limited extent, the central banks of some developing countries extend credits to other developing countries, either directly or through the medium of payments agreements, which they count as reserves (a somewhat dubious statistical procedure, since the balances in question are often illiquid). A projection of $1 billion has been allowed to cover a modest resumption of this practice by 1987.

EXPORT CREDIT EXTENDED BY DEVELOPING COUNTRIES, ETC.

This has been quite a substantial item in the past, and is projected by the IMF at $11.2 billion in 1986. This is a more rapid rebound than seems likely in view of the probable sluggishness of trade among the developing countries, so a figure of $10 billion has been projected for 1987. Of course, this need not represent a net outflow of funds, since many developing-country export credits are financed by banks in developed countries.

BORROWING FROM THE IMF

Drawings from the IMF became a major source of external finance during the recession of the early 1980s and the debt crisis. This development cannot be projected to persist to 1987, however, let alone increase. On the contrary, the IMF deems it important that funds revolve among its members and that it not acquire permanent debtors (de Larosière 1985). By 1987 developing countries will be due to repay nearly $7 billion (gross) from drawings that have already been made. Assuming that new lending by the Fund will offset approaching half of this repayment, net repayments to the Fund of $4 billion can be projected in 1987. This is somewhat less than the Fund's own projection of $5.4 billion net repayments in 1986.

CHANGE IN ARREARS

The arrears built up in 1981–83 are now being worked off. Given our other assumptions, it is likely that this process will be substantially complete by 1987, so the reduction in arrears has been projected at a modest $1 billion.

ERRORS AND OMISSIONS

This item is believed to consist primarily of capital flight. This common interpretation is consistent with the dramatic increase in recorded errors and omissions in 1980–83. The IMF is projecting elimination of this item from 1985 on. This seems mildly optimistic, but not unreasonable, because a reversal of capital flight in some countries could balance continued outflows in others. Thus, it has been adopted as the projection for 1987.

Adequacy of the Prospective Supply of External Finance

The projections derived above are graphed in figure 1 (the column labeled "Projected 1987") and tabulated in table 4, which for convenience also shows actual flows in 1983 (the last year for which all the data are available) and, for each row, the maximum flow recorded up to now. The total projected supply of finance is equal to the current account deficit plus financial needs like reserve building and the extension of export credits.

It would be a mistake to draw much comfort from this equality. At best, it shows only that the growth rate of the developing countries embodied in present forecasts is consistent with the volume of external finance likely to be available. But since this growth rate has been constrained by the expected availability of foreign exchange rather than by the productive potential of the debtor countries, the equality is a confirmation of the feasibility of the forecasts rather than of the adequacy of the supply of external finance. At worst, it must be recalled that the current account forecasts do not make any allowance for adjustment of the US balance of payments or a renewed world recession, and also that bankers have doubts about how easy it will be to reach the projected level of commercial bank lending. The outlook is for external finance to remain tight.

Is it desirable that developing-country growth be restrained to the level of 4 percent to 5 percent in prospect, or would it be better to relax the foreign-exchange constraint? Since the average growth rates for these countries during the two decades prior to the debt crisis approached 6 percent and substantially exceeded the growth rates projected for the next few years, despite the slack that has emerged since 1980, there is a presumption that additional foreign exchange could add significantly to output.

Financial constraints that limit the measured current account deficit on goods, services, and private transfers to $45 billion a year must be judged extremely restrictive. First, one should deduct $16 billion of projected official transfers, to get the more appropriate concept of the current account that measures changes in international net asset positions. Second, with inflation at 3 percent, one should deduct $21 billion for nominal interest payments that will serve simply to compensate for inflationary erosion of the real value of net outstanding debt (some $700 billion)—and 3 percent is a conservative estimate of future inflation. Third, one should recognize that some part of the world's $80-billion-plus measured current account deficit results from unreported earnings, notably of interest, by the residents of developing countries. In fact, it is virtually certain that measured current account deficits of the size currently being recorded and projected for 1987 represent significant real surpluses.[5]

Developing countries have historically run net deficits, and this appears consistent with economic rationality. Of the three fundamental explanations for international borrowing or lending, there is perhaps no particular reason to suppose that the efficient international redistribution of risk requires a systematic flow of capital from rich to poor. Neither need the motive of shifting the distribution of spending over time (for example, to minimize the repercussions of a temporary decline in export receipts) *necessarily* imply a flow to developing countries—although it will be argued below that this should *in fact* be a strong motivation for them to borrow more in the next few years. However, the classic rationale for international capital flows is to redistribute investment from areas where capital productivity is low to those where it is high; and by this criterion it appears paradoxical in the extreme that the developing countries should export rather than import capital and real resources. The normal presumption has always been that rates of return tend to be higher in capital-poor developing countries than in capital-rich developed countries, and therefore that the normal underlying flow of capital should be from the richer countries to the developing countries. The fact that tax breaks led to a faster recovery in investment than normal in the United States in 1982–84 gives no ground for doubting the usual presumption.

Can any rough judgment be made about the level of borrowing that could be considered rational in the ''normal'' situation, when there is no reason to borrow or lend in order to shift expenditures intertemporally? In a world of complete certainty and perfectly enforceable contracts, sufficient capital would flow to equalize yields internationally. Given the actual limited arrangements for the international shifting of risk, however, as well as doubts about the enforceability of contracts, capital flows must be expected to stop far short of this point.

If borrowing is constrained by the risk that debtors will be unable or unwilling to repay, it is natural to examine the measures customarily used to assess the risk of nonperformance by a borrower. The leading contender for this role is the ratio of debt to exports. According to a familiar rule of

---

5. That is, the real (inflation-adjusted) net debt of those countries, deducting their residents' holdings of foreign assets, is declining.

thumb that has received some support from William Cline's (1984 appendix A) logit analysis, a debtor is likely to confront the risk of being forced into rescheduling when its ratio of debt to exports comes to exceed the general range of 200 percent.[6] To avoid this risk, but still be able to borrow to relieve a foreign-exchange shortage, a country should confine its borrowing under normal circumstances to significantly lower ratios of debt to exports.

Ratios of debt to exports can rise very rapidly under adverse circumstances, for example, because a country decides to borrow to sustain its domestic growth when confronted with an external recession that curtails its exports. Using the data of Cline (1984, table E-3), over the period 1973–82, the ratio of debt to exports rose as much as 75 percent in a single year some 5 percent of the time, while over a two-year period it rose as much as 105 percent in a similar proportion of cases. Doubtless these figures are somewhat inflated by instances of countries that ran highly imprudent policies, but they still suggest that a country wishing to limit the risk of being forced to reschedule to less than 5 percent should restrict its normal ratio of debt to exports to no more than 150 percent or so.

In addition to borrowing because real long-term yields of investment are expected to exceed the cost of capital, it is rational for a country to borrow when the value (technically, the shadow price) of foreign exchange exceeds the expected value of foreign exchange in the future by more than the interest rate. This situation arises when a country is so short of foreign exchange that it is forced to limit the level of output to less than full capacity in order to compress imports—a situation traditionally analyzed by the two-gap model (Chenery and Bruno 1962, McKinnon 1964).

The two-gap model derives its name from its recognition of the dual role that an inflow of external finance can play, in adding both to the supply of savings (so reducing the "savings gap") and to the supply of foreign exchange (thus reducing the "foreign-exchange gap"). The model treats the extreme case where production requires the input of some intermediate good, in a fixed ratio to output, as well as a combination of two distinct types of capital goods in fixed proportions, only one of which can be made at home. The model is discussed by Williamson (1983, chapter 12.3) and Bergsten, Cline, and Williamson (1985, appendix).

---

6. The analogous econometric estimates of McFadden et al. (1985) also find a clear role for the ratio of debt to exports in precipitating debt problems, but this study finds sufficient other relevant significant variables as to preclude drawing even weak support for such a simple rule of thumb.

The central conclusion of the two-gap model is that the productivity of foreign exchange in terms of increasing domestic growth can depend, perhaps drastically, upon whether or not the economy is constrained by a shortage of foreign exchange from operating at full capacity. When foreign exchange is sufficiently plentiful to permit purchase of all the intermediate inputs and capital goods that are demanded at full capacity but cannot be produced at home, additional foreign exchange simply permits a relaxation of the savings constraint, and therefore a rise in investment[7] equal to the increase in foreign borrowing. The productivity of foreign borrowing is far higher when the economy is constrained to operate at less than full capacity by a shortage of foreign exchange. By allowing extra domestic production (and not simply extra *absorption*), and therefore generating higher domestic savings, additional foreign borrowing can support a bigger addition to investment than in the savings-constrained case, *plus* a rise in consumption.

There are two main criticisms of the two-gap model. One is that it is too rigid in assuming that import coefficients are fixed and that exports are exogenous. But it is possible to recognize that, in the longer run, import substitution and export promotion are feasible[8] without rejecting the central insight of the two-gap model, that the productivity of extra foreign exchange is much higher when the foreign-exchange constraint is binding. The possibility of adjustment simply implies that the foreign-exchange constraint can be relaxed in the long run to the point where it ceases to bind, through pursuit of appropriate policies—not that it *never* binds. Indeed, the possibility of adjusting the current account in the longer run (which means that foreign borrowing can be repaid more easily later on) forms the basis for the contention that it is rational to borrow to ease the foreign-exchange constraint. If the constraint were not temporary, the loss of output at the time of repayment would equal the gain at the time of borrowing and borrowing would give no net advantage.

A more difficult issue is posed by the hypothesis of a sharp switch point between savings-constrained and exchange-constrained regimes. In economic contexts, a progressive switch from one regime to another is more common than a sharp break. A break perhaps occurs in the present context because of the influence of a third constraint on the level of activity that is ignored

---

7. Or some part of the borrowing may be consumed rather than invested.

8. Indeed, these are the prime objectives of the adjustment programs being pursued in most debtor countries.

by the two-gap model, namely the rate (or acceleration) of inflation. If one postulates that the rate of inflation is a positive function of the level of activity and of competitiveness (as measured by the real exchange rate), and that inflation must not be allowed to accelerate, then it follows that, as capacity utilization increases, a part of any increased foreign-exchange availability has to be utilized in allowing a real appreciation rather than in increasing output through the multiplier formula of the two-gap model. Moreover, if this proportion increases as full capacity utilization is approached (according to the customary hypothesis that inflationary pressure mounts progressively as output approaches capacity), the transition toward the situation depicted in the model of the fully employed, savings-constrained economy will be gradual (Bergsten, Cline, and Williamson 1985, appendix).

Such a gradual transition implies that a rational government should give gradually decreasing weight to conserving foreign exchange as its balance of payments position improves. Initially, the bulk of a payments improvement should be utilized to increase output toward full capacity, but as this objective is approached there should be an increasing emphasis on reducing the ratio of debt to exports toward the prudent level of (perhaps) 150 percent.

At the present time most developing countries appear to be constrained by a shortage of foreign exchange. Table 2 showed projected debtor-country growth rates substantially below the historical norm. While it is likely that the potential growth rates for these economies have been reduced somewhat by the rise in real interest rates and other shifts in relative prices, it seems unlikely that they have fallen as much as the projected growth rates have. Moreover, many countries are starting from a position of substantial excess capacity as a result of the austerity of the early and mid-1980s. At the same time, ratios of debt to exports are projected to be improving (table 5). Hence, both fundamental conditions that are necessary to justify borrowing to relieve a foreign-exchange constraint will be satisfied. A larger capital flow than seems likely would be desirable from the standpoint of the debtors. Moreover, the rest of the world would surely welcome expanded export opportunities in the markets of the developing countries.

The time profile of the demand for external finance envisaged here is at variance with what the bankers appear willing to supply. Economics suggests that the need for external finance is greatest in the short run, before expenditure switching can be fully effective. Once adjustment has occurred, debtors would be well-advised to hoard their reestablished creditworthiness against the eventuality of a new deterioration in the global environment. Bankers, however, seem willing to envisage an enlargement of lending (though not to

TABLE 5   **Ratio of net debt to exports, 19 major debtors, 1983 and 1987**

Country	1983	Projected 1987
Algeria	0.8	0.6
Argentina	4.9	3.2
Brazil	3.7	2.3
Chile	3.1	1.5
Ecuador	2.4	3.1
Egypt	2.1	0.9
Hungary	0.6	0.5
Indonesia	1.0	2.1
Israel	2.3	2.2
Korea	1.2	0.6
Mexico	3.1	2.1
Peru	2.8	4.0
Philippines	3.1	2.4
Portugal	2.2	2.1
Romania	0.6	−0.1
Thailand	1.0	0.8
Turkey	2.1	1.4
Venezuela	1.5	1.1
Yugoslavia	1.3	0.9
Average	2.0	1.4

Source: Cline, *International Debt,* tables 8.2–8.4.

the levels of the 1970s) once the adjustment process is complete, but not before.

This argument can be illustrated diagrammatically (figure 2). The line AEF represents the path of external debt that the economy can comfortably service: to a first approximation it may be assumed to rise steadily as productive potential and export opportunities expand.[9] BCD represents the stylized path that debt accumulation has taken from the first oil shock to the present day. Starting from a position B where debt was significantly below the level that

---

9. It would be more accurate to recognize that the sustainable debt path is endogenous with respect to both the global environment and the policies of the debtor countries. For example, the world recession and high interest rates of the early 1980s shifted the trajectory down and thus helped precipitate the debt crisis. Nevertheless, the contrast illustrated in the figure can be seen more clearly if these qualifications are neglected.

FIGURE 2 **Alternative visions of optimal borrowing**

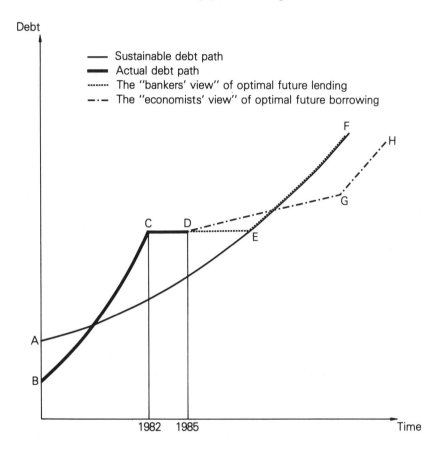

could be serviced, countries started to build up debt at a rate that was faster than sustainable. The recession of the early 1980s brought this fact home: the drying up of new lending in mid-1982 precipitated the debt crisis. Since then, the real debt buildup of developing countries has effectively ceased, as documented above.

What we have characterized as the "bankers' view" holds that this is desirable, and that these countries should not borrow further until they have returned to the sustainable debt trajectory at point E, which they may reach by the early 1990s, whereupon they should resume borrowing at the sustainable rate. The "economists' view" (our own) is quite different. First, because output is constrained by a shortage of foreign exchange, it is desirable to borrow more now in order to raise output closer to productive potential over the next few years. Second, because of the costs of not being able to borrow more to insulate the economy in the short run against adverse exogenous shocks, it is desirable to seek a long-run debt path like GH *below* the sustainable path. Putting those two points together, the optimal path is DGH, involving a prompt resumption of borrowing (though at a rate below the sustainable rate), but the maintenance of a restrained rate of borrowing for a relatively long time (perhaps another decade).

What might be meant by a "restrained rate of borrowing"? To form some benchmark estimate, start with the IMF's forecast that exports of goods and services of nonoil developing countries will reach $564 billion in 1986 (IMF 1985, appendix table 37). This suggests that the exports of those countries in 1987 will exceed $600 billion. Using the rule of thumb suggested earlier, that the optimal ratio of debt to exports might be about 150 percent, but recognizing that many countries will wish to maintain lower debt levels, suggests a sustainable debt level of around $800 billion in 1987. This sustainable debt level would grow at perhaps 8 percent a year (3 percent for inflation and 5 percent for the trend real growth rate of the developing countries), or by some $64 billion a year. To that must be added $16 billion in official transfers, to get the sustainable current account deficit on the IMF definition: $80 billion. Thus, even without making any allowance for unrecorded current account receipts, the projected current account deficit is not much over half the steady-state deficit. A "restrained rate of borrowing" might reasonably be interpreted as one that halved the gap between the prospective and steady-state deficits; i.e., borrowing of some $15 billion to $20 billion more each year than is in prospect on current projections for the remainder of the decade.

Additional borrowing of $20 billion a year would permit a rise in output on the order of $100 billion, since marginal import propensities are typically perhaps 20 percent, and output is currently constrained by the shortage of foreign exchange. The extra output could and typically would be used to increase both current consumption and investment, which would provide the potential for faster future growth. Actually realizing that additional growth in the future will require extra foreign exchange. If enough of the investment is used to increase export capacity, export-led growth will supply the needed foreign exchange. Extra borrowing cannot substitute for export-led growth, but it will be a boon if used to promote it.

Would not extra borrowing of $40 billion permit twice as many benefits? Gross benefits might well be twice as great, since wasted resources are surely more than $200 billion a year. But a strategy that foregoes, as this would, short-run progress toward restoring creditworthiness is simply too risky, even if it were viable. Additional borrowing of $15 billion to $20 billion a year for the rest of the decade is, in contrast, a target that would clearly benefit the debtors while ensuring that if events turn out as anticipated they will make good progress toward restoring creditworthiness.

Of course, events do not always turn out as anticipated. But that merely reinforces the argument for seeking to expand capital flows to the developing countries. On present prospects, any net worsening in their payments situation will compel them to cut back their growth even further below the rate that is permitted by the supply side. Better access to the world capital market can diminish that danger.

Borrowing of $50 billion a year rather than the $30 billion-odd that is likely on present projections (after deducting official transfers) would be a drop in the ocean when compared to the total size or the rate of increase in the size of world capital markets. As of 1980, for example, the total capitalization of major world markets for bonds, equities, precious metals, and mortgages exceeded $11.5 trillion (Ibbotson and Siegel 1983). The annual increase in this sum (including capital appreciation as well as new savings flows) is substantially in excess of $1 trillion. Clearly the volume of capital available to developing countries is not going to be limited by the pool of funds available, but rather by perceptions of the borrowers' creditworthiness. (In 1981, before those perceptions deteriorated, developing countries borrowed over $80 billion on private markets.) Since those perceptions will be influenced by the structure of borrowing, it is time to pass to the next topic.

3   The Structure of External Finance

This section deals with the principles on which international finance should be restructured if a more efficient international distribution of risk and a more appropriate distribution over time of debt-service obligations is to be achieved. The purpose of this restructuring is to permit greater exploitation through financial transactions of comparative advantage in risk bearing, in the same way that the international trading system permits the exploitation of comparative advantage in the production of goods. We argue later that this was not achieved in the 1970s because the borrowers seriously underestimated the magnitude of the risks to which they were exposed.

As noted in the introduction, most nonconcessional external finance secured by developing countries has taken one of two forms: either direct investment, in which the investor retains control of the investment and participates fully in its profits and losses, or general obligation financing, in which the lender provides money to be repaid on terms independent of the success of the investment made with the funds thus supplied. In recent years, general obligation borrowing, typically in the form of floating-rate commercial bank loans, has come to dominate, accounting for as much as 70 percent of new nonconcessional financing during the peak borrowing years in the late 1970s and early 1980s.

The section starts with a discussion of the desirable attributes of international finance and how these differ depending on the situation of the borrowing country. It then examines the advantages and shortcomings of the two major types of nonconcessional financing that have historically been available to developing countries: floating-rate bank loans and direct foreign investment.

Desirable Attributes

At the most basic level, international finance can benefit a country by enabling it to increase and stabilize its income over time and across circumstances. It allows the country to undertake investments whose prospective returns exceed the costs of finance, which it would have to forego or postpone if it had to depend on its own savings or foreign-exchange generation. When the foreign-exchange constraint is not binding, foreign capital simply substitutes for or adds to domestic savings, and hence shifts absorption one for one. It also allows the country to increase (postpone) its absorption of resources in periods where additional consumption or investment has a particularly high (low) value compared to future periods either because of expected trends in income or because of internal or external shocks. When the foreign-exchange constraint is binding, as noted above in discussion of the two-gap model, foreign finance can increase the level of production, and hence increase income over time as well as stabilize it.[10]

---

10. For a more complete discussion of the various uses of external finance, including country examples, see World Bank (1985, chapter 4).

Of course, international finance can also play a perverse role by allowing governments to postpone necessary adjustments, undertake projects whose prospective returns do not justify the resources invested and the risks involved, or neglect the mobilization of domestic savings. All of these occurred in the great developing-country borrowing spree of 1974–81. In retrospect, it is obvious that much of the borrowing of that period shifted absorption forward to a time when foreign exchange was in less short supply than it is now, and thus decreased welfare for the reasons explained by the two-gap model. It is also conventional wisdom now that some of the borrowing (though perhaps less than is believed by the typical denigrator of the banks and developing countries) was misused on armaments, capital flight, or prestige projects. A part of a policy to prevent any repetition of such follies has to be better macroeconomic and microeconomic (project appraisal and performance incentive) policies of the borrowers; but a better structuring of international finance can help, too.

Assuming that the resources obtained through external finance are put to good use, the desirability of a particular mix of financing arrangements depends on the extent to which they help the country achieve its goals of increasing and stabilizing income. This depends on four elements:

- cash-flow matching

- performance incentives

- impact on local financial markets

- contract enforceability.

These dimensions are discussed in turn below.

CASH-FLOW MATCHING

Since external finance involves the receipt of foreign exchange in the present in exchange for an obligation to repay foreign exchange in the future, the form of this obligation has a great deal to do with the benefit a country can achieve from external finance. In very general terms, if financing takes the form of general obligation borrowing, it involves a commitment to repay an amount of foreign exchange that in principle is independent of the condition of the domestic economy. Thus, the same debt service will be due when foreign exchange is scarce as when it is not. If servicing obligations take the form of a share of net foreign-exchange earnings, in contrast, repayments will be smallest when foreign exchange is scarcest, and vice versa. Clearly, finance giving rise to obligations keyed to a country's capacity to pay contributes more to its objectives, other things being equal, and hence a country should be willing to pay a somewhat higher expected cost for such financing.

The cost of external financing must be interpreted broadly to reflect not only the amount of the promised or expected repayment in relation to the amount borrowed, but also its timing and coincidence with other circumstances affecting a country's overall income and consumption. The least costly form of nonconcessional finance in terms of expected payments is likely to be general obligation bank borrowing or floating rate notes, where the borrower promises to pay a specified spread over short-term market rates regardless of its own circumstances. However, to the extent that upswings in interest rates and hence debt service coincide with a worsening of the borrower's overall foreign-exchange situation, either because the factors giving rise to these swings tend to coincide with factors depressing demand for its exports or because of its other interest-bearing foreign obligations, such financing will involve relatively large payments when foreign exchange is scarcest. Borrowing with an interest-rate cap, in contrast, might be more costly on average, since lenders would charge a risk premium for the interest-rate insurance implicit in the cap, but it might be less "costly" in terms of the borrowing country's general well-being since payments would be limited in periods where market rates are very high and, as a result, the borrower is under a great deal of financial pressure. The expected cost of financing involving an equity claim on a particular activity is likely to be even higher, but its "cost" in terms of the borrowing country's well-being might be comparable or lower than the cost of bank credit since the largest payments would be likely to be due when times are good for the borrowing country.

Because borrowing countries and investors who participate in world capital markets differ in the risks to which they are exposed, they will possess comparative advantage in bearing particular risks. Because the economies of Nigeria or Venezuela, for example, are much more exposed to shifts in energy prices than the world economy as a whole, they should be able to gain by laying off some of these risks through financing arrangements. This comparative advantage will be reflected in the fact that the premium demanded by world investors for bearing oil price risks will be substantially lower than the premium such countries should be willing to pay to avoid them. In contrast, oil importers such as Brazil or Korea would benefit from financing arrangements that relate debt-service payments inversely to oil prices.[11] One of the major problems with developing-country borrowing decisions in the 1970s was that borrowers underestimated the risks associated with their income from the production of primary commodities, and hence did not give sufficient weight to the impact of alternative financing arrangements on the volatility of their income net of debt service.

Furthermore, because of domestic rigidities, developing countries can easily become foreign-exchange constrained, which gives them a greater effective exposure to variations in real and nominal interest rates than industrial country borrowers or lenders. This exposure will be reinforced to the extent that variations in world interest rates or the exchange rates of currencies in which they borrow coincide with variations in their foreign-exchange earnings before debt service. As a result, developing countries will, other things being equal, benefit from financial terms that limit their exposure to such variations.

Several features of financial arrangements determine the extent to which required foreign-exchange payments correspond to the borrower's capacity to pay. These include degree of risk sharing and hedging, continuity, time matching, and flexibility.

Risk sharing occurs when debt-service obligations are linked explicitly to some aspect of the borrower's economic situation. Equity investment, for example, entitles the investor to a pro rata share of the profits of a particular firm, while commodity-linked bonds or export participation notes perform the same role at the level of the economy as a whole. This attribute is most valuable to a borrower when the shared risks contribute significantly to the variability of income or the availability of foreign exchange, or both. The outstanding examples are countries whose exports are dominated by one or two primary products, such as Chile and Zambia (copper) or Ecuador and Nigeria (oil).

Since countries and investors have comparative advantages in bearing different risks, the gains from risk sharing often depend on the extent to which the various risks entailed in a specific activity can be unbundled and assigned to the party best able to bear them. As we shall show below, the

---

11. It is sometimes suggested that countries could hedge key commodity price exposures by borrowing in the currency of a country with similar exposures to key commodities. An oil exporter, for example, might wish to borrow sterling, given its role as a petrocurrency, while an oil importer might wish to borrow yen, given Japan's adverse exposure to oil price increases. While such currency selection would represent a move in the right direction, it would typically provide only a very partial hedge, since many other factors in addition to the relative prices of commodities influence exchange rates, as witnessed by the recent gyrations of sterling.

desirable specificity of the contract depends not only on each party's exposure to various risks but also on the effect of specificity on incentives and contract enforceability.

Hedging reflects the extent to which variations in the costs of financing resulting from shifts in external economic variables, such as interest rates and exchange rates, correspond to shifts in a country's income or ability to pay. If a country's terms of trade, for example, tend to worsen with real appreciation of the dollar versus, say, the European currency unit (ECU), then ECU financing will serve as a hedge.[12] In contrast, if a country's terms of trade tend to worsen when nominal interest rates increase, which would be the case in a world economy dominated by supply shocks, floating-rate debt would be a poor choice because it would represent a doubling up rather than hedging of exposure.[13] It is clear that implementation of such a hedging strategy will require substantial knowledge of the structure of the economy and careful empirical testing of covariances, with care taken to rely only on relationships that appear robust. Hedging may be possible through the purchase of options or through entry into swap contracts, in which case risk management can be divorced from the supply of capital (section 4).

The degree of *continuity* of finance refers to the presence or absence of interruptions in the supply of finance to a particular borrower. This combines two elements: the continuity of supply of funds in general and the availability of those funds to the borrower in question. Any single source of funds is subject to interruption. In the case of commercial bank loans, for example, interruption may result from disintermediation that reduces the global supply of bank loans, or shifts in bank policy or regulation toward developing countries. Floating-rate credit supplied for a fixed term is, in essence, a guarantee of access to a particular quantity of funds at the current short-term rate plus a constant spread. Commercial borrowers typically seek to maintain continuity through contractual arrangements such as lines of credit and by maintaining borrowing relationships with a variety of sources. Continuity is most important to countries that need to borrow to stabilize consumption, for example because of fluctuating export receipts, or which face high costs of postponing investment outlays.

The *time matching* of financing refers to the degree to which the time

---

12. See World Bank (1985, especially box 3.1) for further discussion.

13. The World Bank (1985, box 3.2) stresses the opposite circumstance, a world economy dominated by demand shocks, with the opposite conclusions. This underscores the difficulty of hedging with instruments that are only indirectly linked to a country's income or ability to pay.

profile of repayment obligations matches the profile of resources available for debt service. The usual rule of thumb is that long-term projects should be financed by loans with equivalent maturities, while current trade activities can be financed with short-term obligations. However, at the country level the matching should be in terms of ability to pay at the aggregate level, which has little to do with the maturity of the assets being financed. In practice, time matching requires spreading debt service as equally as possible over future periods where foreign-exchange surpluses or ready access to new financing or both are anticipated and, in particular, avoiding the bunching of maturities.

A country embarking on a major development program with a substantial gestation period, for example, will want a repayment schedule with a substantial grace period followed by level or perhaps rising real debt service over the anticipated surplus years. Much railroad building in the Americas was financed with 99-year bonds in the last century! Financial markets typically do not provide such financing nowadays, especially with high and volatile inflation, so the best a country can do is to stretch its repayments over enough years to give it a reasonable chance of refinancing without a repayment crisis. In the case of countries at an early stage of development, the prospect of net debt-service payments being made is so distant as virtually to preclude the utilization of commercial finance, no matter how high the prospective rate of return.

A country borrowing to facilitate its adjustment to a temporary external shock, in contrast, might be quite willing to accept projected repayments over a relatively short period of time. The importance of this attribute for specific borrowers depends on their expected time profiles of income, as well as on their ability to alter the timing of consumption and investment to maintain debt service.

Flexibility of finance refers to the flexibility both of supply and of repayment in the face of unforeseen events. It is a partial substitute for both continuity and time matching, since flexibility in repayment reduces the premium a country will place on continuity in the supply of new financing and before-the-fact matching of its debt service and its capacity to pay.

PERFORMANCE INCENTIVES

In addition to shifting risks, and thus stabilizing a borrower's income over time, financing whose cost is linked to specified circumstances may have important incentive effects which can increase a country's expected level of income or reduce its variability. When debt-service obligations are linked to the outcomes of specific projects or undertakings with limited recourse to a country's general credit, foreign lenders or investors obtain a stake in the success of the project. This linkage may improve performance and reduce risk when lenders or investors have some control over variables crucial to a project's success. For example, if all or part of the yield on an obligation is tied to the performance of the project financed, the vendor has a greater interest in seeing that the project design is appropriate and its management is satisfactory. Similarly, if the obligations of a borrowing country were linked to its volume of manufactured exports, lenders would have a greater interest in assuring that country's continued access to markets for its products. However, if the potential lenders do not have control over variables relevant to the project's success, the main impact of linking debt-service obligations to outcomes is likely to be in the credit analysis undertaken before the loan is made. If the project is not robust, i.e., able to generate returns sufficient to pay debt service under most plausible exogenous circumstances, a project-finance structure is likely to lead lenders not to provide finance at all.

The incentive effects of any financial contract depend on its *specificity* in terms of risk sharing. Because an equity share is specific to a particular firm, it gives financiers an incentive to promote that firm's success. Because a production-share or risk-service contract, typically employed on oil and gas projects, links investor returns to a narrower measure of project success, it focuses incentives on managing those dimensions appropriately. General obligation borrowing, in contrast, is not linked to any particular project or risk dimension and hence provides lenders with a stake only in a country's overall foreign-exchange situation.

In cases where a foreign investor can add significantly to the value of an undertaking through its knowledge base or access to markets, some form of stakeholding will be beneficial. But in cases where domestic policy choices are the primary determinant of project success or failure, such foreign participation will confront moral hazard. The risk of self-serving government policies will tend to confound the incentives facing the foreign investor and reduce the credibility of the contract, a point explored below. Since most activities involve both types of risks, it can be beneficial to separate them in contracting. This point is further developed in the discussion of quasi-equity instruments.

IMPACT ON LOCAL FINANCIAL MARKETS

International finance can never be more than a complement to domestic savings, and it typically will be available on the best terms and employed most usefully when it is accompanied by healthy domestic capital formation. A major problem in many developing countries is insufficient capital formation; indeed, capital flight has been a principal contributor to a number of countries' external financial crises. This poor record reflects both unattractive climates for domestic savings—high taxes, negative real interest rates, fears of confiscation, discrimination against nonbank financial intermediaries, and regulations limiting the scope of investment—and distortions in foreign-exchange markets that create arbitrage opportunities that outweigh potential domestic returns.

International finance in the form of general obligation borrowing has allowed developing-country governments to bypass local financial markets. As a result, many of the policy measures necessary to stimulate domestic capital formation have been neglected. Certain forms of international finance, in contrast, especially portfolio investment in corporate equities and bonds, make use of domestic markets and hence will be successful only to the extent that these markets flourish.

These three dimensions—cash-flow matching, performance incentives, and impact on local financial markets—determine which financing arrangements are desirable for a country. However, not all desirable contracts are feasible, given the difficulty of creating credible and enforceable contracts across national boundaries.

CONTRACT ENFORCEABILITY

While an obligation to pay a share of its foreign-exchange earnings would be ideal in terms of matching repayments with a country's capacity to pay, such a contract has other disadvantages, as a result of which it is unlikely that finance would be available on this basis. A major disadvantage is that such a contract would confront serious moral hazard, since a country's foreign-exchange earnings depend to a large extent on its own actions.

Contracts across borders are harder to enforce than those between two parties within one jurisdiction. A sovereign can reject a claim against itself within its own territory (although there are cases where parastatals have foresworn such rights), and the sanctions that can be applied elsewhere are limited by legal and practical considerations. Further, a sovereign has considerable discretion over policy choices that influence its own or its citizens' ability to fulfill the contract. Thus, the parameters of control of one party become the elements of risk for the other party.

This ability of governments to influence economic outcomes, coupled with a lender's limited scope for imposing legal sanctions, means that contracts between developing countries and the private market have little economic value unless both parties feel that it is in their long-term interest to honor their obligations. An "obsolescent bargain" will have to be revised if the creditor is to avoid repudiation of his rights (Vernon 1971). The countries most likely to meet their commitments are those that would suffer most if they did not do so, both in terms of the likelihood that particular sanctions will be brought to bear and the cost to the country of these sanctions.

The principal sanctions that can be imposed on a sovereign borrower in the case of nonperformance are the withholding of future finance and the blocking of commercial transactions that would put national assets at risk of seizure. Thus, the costs to a borrower of nonperformance will depend on the importance of its future trade and finance with the country or countries that will honor the lenders' claim. In the case of commercial bank lending, these may include most potential lenders because of the formal and informal network among banks and their respective governments. In the case of an equity investment, in contrast, the prospect for a concerted response may be considerably less. This is especially likely if nonperformance takes the form of "creeping expropriation," that is, policy shifts that reduce the value of the equity investment but do not involve outright expropriation (Bergsten, Horst, and Moran 1978).

In some cases, these limits to enforceability can be overcome at a cost. In extractive projects, for example, it is common to locate downstream and primary production facilities in different countries to reduce the value of the primary stages in the event of expropriation. The costs of this arrangement are additional transportation charges and other departures from economic efficiency. In other cases, a project may have to be oriented toward export markets even though economic efficiency would dictate home use to attract financing, to enable the proceeds to be captured by lenders. China's recent offshore gas discovery provides a case in point: lenders are reportedly pressing for the gas to be exported to Japan. Even when efficiency dictates exporting the project's output, the legal arrangements for "earmarking" the proceeds have a cost in that they create senior debt obligations that reduce the country's overall financial flexibility and, consequently, the enforceability of its general obligations. In the extreme, these limits to enforceability will be such that no financing takes place, in which case the cost is the foregone economic benefit of the project.

The specificity of a contract is often a significant factor in its enforceability. General obligations gain their credibility from the fact that nonperformance on one is likely to trigger a cutoff of all others. Nonperformance on more specific contracts, in contrast, is less likely to trigger a collective lender response, so their credibility depends on the ability of the creditor to impose sanctions in the form of legal seizure of specific foreign-exchange proceeds or the denial of further access to critical inputs or information. Thus, a contract to develop an oil field for export may be highly credible, whereas one to develop an identical field in another country that will use the output to reduce its dependence on imports may be even less credible than a general obligation of the same country, since it will be subject to the risk of output pricing (for example, that prices will be depressed by price controls) as well as to general transfer risk. This is ironic since the incremental oil production, assuming similar geological and technological characteristics, is more valuable to the latter country (because of savings in transport costs and the fact that its exposure to variations in world oil prices is diminished rather than amplified).

Financial contracts across national boundaries face a hierarchy of risks. All contracts, with the exception of those involving an escrowing of specified foreign-exchange earnings, are exposed to transfer risk—the risk that the country will not have and make available the foreign exchange to service the debt. Transfer risk involves both elements of chance, such as variations in interest rates and terms of trade directly affecting a country's *ability* to pay, and elements of choice, such as macroeconomic policies which reflect the country's *willingness* to pay. This dual character of transfer risk is a major barrier to writing enforceable contracts across borders, since it may be difficult to determine if nonperformance results from chance or choice.

General obligations face only this risk (apart from the minimal risk that a country will repudiate its debts out of ideology or calculations of net worth). Obligations denominated in currencies other than those of the borrowing country, but payable in its jurisdiction, are also subject to the risk of exchange controls, as holders of Mex-dollar deposits and Mexican petro-bonds learned to their dismay. Debt contracts denominated in the local currency, of course, are also subject to the risk of inflation and devaluation. In addition, equity investments or loans to specific companies or projects are subject to the commercial risks of the firm or project. These commercial risks include elements under managerial control, but they also include the exposure of these firms or projects to policy measures the country may adopt in managing its economy or to policy measures of other countries. Examples of the former are the austerity measures adopted by developing countries in response to their debt crises, which have thrown many local firms into severe financial crises of their own. Examples of the latter are protectionist policies which threaten export markets. Thus, in many cases, there is no clear dividing line between noncommercial risks and commercial risks.

In general, the presence of significant transfer risks will drive out specific financing that does not bypass this risk via escrowing of foreign-exchange proceeds in offshore accounts. This denies the country the possible risk sharing and incentive benefits of such contracts. The resulting void may be partially filled by multilateral development bank (MDB) guarantees or other investment insurance schemes that cover investors against noncommercial risks and, as in the case of the proposed Multilateral Investment Guarantee Authority (MIGA), subject nonperformance on a specific investment contract to similar treatment as nonperformance on a general obligation.

An example can illustrate the type of role that an MDB (or national agencies, such as the Overseas Private Investment Corporation, OPIC, in the United States) could play in overcoming output-pricing and transfer risks. Consider again the example of a project producing energy for the domestic market. A requirement that domestic prices be linked by formula to world prices could be incorporated in a project loan covenant and monitored by an MDB (or OPIC). Transfer risk could be covered by an MDB or OPIC through a guarantee which could be called only if the borrower had generated the local currency but was unable to obtain foreign exchange from its central bank. Thus, the foreign investor would be enabled to exploit its comparative advantage in assessing and executing energy projects.

In this regard, MIGA is particularly interesting since it would entail an agreement among investors and host countries to provide guarantees to qualifying investments against various noncommercial risks. The critical distinction between MIGA and existing public or private insurance schemes is that it would provide a mechanism for monitoring agreements and imposing sanctions in cases of violations by contracting parties. Given the large element of choice underlying most noncommercial risks, therefore, it would address a major imbalance in the current international financial system. The viability of the current system depends to a great extent on the leverage of the IMF and the World Bank vis-à-vis developing countries. This leverage results from the fact that these institutions are a continuing source of finance that plays a special role in signaling to other financial institutions whether or not to continue lending to a particular country.[14] To date, these institutions have

---

14. The rapid movement of the World Bank toward structural adjustment loans in the face of declining project lending possibilities can be interpreted as a move to maintain self-enforceability by holding out future net lending as a reward to countries that meet their current obligations.

applied this leverage to maintain the credibility of general obligation borrowings, but not of direct or portfolio investment.[15]

In fact, the measures imposed by the IMF in conjunction with commercial banks often have the effect of imposing losses on holders of corporate debt or equity in order to increase the ability of the debtor country to meet its sovereign, general obligations. Thus, it is not surprising that the structure of international financing for developing countries has shifted toward general obligation lending to sovereigns. The whole area of how central banks appear to allocate scarce foreign exchange as between private and public creditors and debt and equity claimants, even outside of a rescheduling situation, is an interesting one. There appears to be an implicit hierarchy involving an anti-private, anti-equity bias that militates against portfolio and direct investors. This point certainly deserves greater attention. We believe that MDBs can play a major role in redressing this imbalance and that MIGA could provide a focal point to support the other types of financing we have discussed. This would not only make developing countries less vulnerable to world crises, but it would also inject many more market incentives into the selection and management of specific projects, thus aiding developing-country governments in a quest for realistic and dynamic policies.

Appraisal of the Current Structure: Bank Borrowing

As noted, general obligation borrowing, largely in the form of floating-rate commercial bank loans, came to dominate the nonconcessional financing of developing countries in the 1970s. While borrowing from banks on a general obligation basis has some clear advantages, it also has several drawbacks and several characteristics that may either be beneficial or detrimental, depending on circumstances. Its primary advantages are its apparent low cost and its after-the-fact flexibility. Its clear disadvantages are its lack of risk shifting, its poor hedge characteristics, and its undermining of local capital markets.

Two key characteristics that can cut either way are the nonspecific nature of bank lending and its concentration in relatively few, homogeneous lending institutions. Its nonspecific nature derives from the fact that almost all bank

---

15. The United States and various other investor countries attempt to impose sanctions in the case of expropriation of direct holdings. However, these mechanisms typically are not very effective because of the difficulty of determining damages and assigning fault, and hence obtaining the collective response required to make the penalties effective.

loans to developing countries are explicitly or implicitly general obligations of the borrowing country.[16] This is a positive feature in that it has allowed borrowers to maintain complete control over the use of the borrowed funds. But it is a negative feature in that it does not involve foreign lenders or investors taking a stake in project or enterprise outcomes.

Its general obligation nature, plus its concentration in relatively few lending institutions, are positive factors in that they have in general enhanced the enforceability of developing-country obligations, and thus have made credit available where it otherwise might not have been. They have also made possible after-the-fact flexibility in terms of debt rescheduling, thus mitigating the perverse hedging and time-matching characteristics of bank lending. However, this concentration of loans also exposes developing countries to variations in the supply of funds due to changes in banks' financial conditions and regulatory constraints, as well as to changes in attitude on the part of a handful of individuals. Further, this concentration has the potential to transform a developing-country repayment crisis into a crisis for the world financial system to a much greater extent than might otherwise be the case. These points are elaborated in the remainder of this section.

APPARENT LOW COST

In the heyday of bank lending, bank financing was available at much lower rates than long-term bond financing and even World Bank financing denominated in the same currency. Further, at then-current rates of inflation, these borrowing rates were close to zero in real terms. If considered in terms of a borrowing country's well-being, though, this cost advantage was illusory. Since bank borrowing is a general obligation linked to short-term rates, it *should* bear a lower rate on average than most other forms of finance in order to present a competitive cost-risk mix.

A true cost advantage, however, derives from its relatively greater enforceability. This enforceability, in turn, is the result of two factors, the recurring nature of general obligation borrowing from banks and the potential for collective action by them. When few external sanctions can be imposed, contract enforceability is greatest when there are recurring transactions, since

---

16. Even in the case of nonguaranteed loans to private firms or banks, foreign lenders have been able to coerce the borrowers' governments into taking responsibility for the obligations. In some cases, the governments in question assumed the loans; in others they put into place special policies, such as dual exchange rates, that had the effect of transferring resources to the firms to allow them to meet their external obligations.

nonperformance on any one contract will lead to the loss of many subsequent ones. In such cases a borrower builds a reputation over time by honoring its commitments and must weigh the loss of this reputation and its impact on future borrowings against the benefit of defaulting.

The concentration of lending to developing countries on relatively few banks implies that ongoing trade and finance will involve a fairly steady stream of transactions and, hence, high implicit costs for nonperformance. In contrast, a firm with a one-shot investment or a group of bondholders have a less continuing relationship and, as a result, a weaker position.

Since the enforceability of international financial claims against developing countries depends upon sanctions such as a cutoff of future trade or finance in the case of default, it depends upon the potential for a collective response by lenders. Because all bank debt of a given country involves the same type of general obligations, there is relatively little conflict of interest among banks. Further, the banks have evolved collaborative mechanisms in the event of repayment crises to minimize any playing off of one bank against another by the borrower.

DEBT-SERVICE MISMATCH

Most developing countries experience fluctuations in revenue due to world economic cycles, shifts in the terms of trade, and domestic political and economic events. International finance should aid the smoothing of national consumption over time, through borrowing in periods of low income and replenishing reserves or repaying debt in periods of high income. However, if a country already has substantial external obligations, it may have difficulty borrowing more, and indeed the obligation to service its existing debt may rise and intensify the fluctuation in its underlying level of income. Thus, it will desire financing that matches its ability to pay over time and in response to various shocks in the world economy. Commercial bank finance does neither.

Most commercial bank loans are of relatively short maturity. Five to seven years is viewed as being long term; many loans are for only one to three years, and they typically require full debt service from the outset. Further, the debt service usually involves level repayments of principal, which implies a path of debt service in real terms that declines over time as a function of the rate of inflation in the currency in which the loan is contracted. An increase in inflation effectively accelerates the required debt service and shortens the weighted average maturity, or "duration," of the loan.

In a world with perfect information and complete enforceability, the part of the perverse variation in debt service due to fluctuations in inflation would not be a problem. Claims would be rolled over unless the present value of a borrowing country's future net exports fell short of the present value of outstanding claims. In other words, illiquidity would never be an issue and the only risk would be that of insolvency. However, given limited information and enforceability, rolling over is not a sure thing, and the short and uncertain effective maturities of floating-rate loans can create problems for borrowers as well as for the system as a whole.

The repayment profile of bank financing shifts with changes in current, short-term interest rates that reflect changes in anticipated inflation as well as changes in real interest rates. Over the recent past, such increases in real rates have tended to coincide with a worsening of the economic situation of developing countries. While this relationship may change in the future, since a more traditional expectation is that interest rates will tend to rise during a world boom when export earnings are strong, the recent experience has been that variations in the cost of bank borrowing have exacerbated rather than ameliorated fluctuations in borrowing countries' incomes. This problem has been offset to some extent by after-the-fact reschedulings of debt-service obligations, but this process has been costly to all parties involved.

LIMITED RISK SHARING AND SHIFTING OF RESPONSIBILITY

Most commercial bank loans to developing countries and all World Bank loans involve explicit or implicit government guarantees. Thus, while the funds may be earmarked for a specific project or program, their repayment is not contingent on that project's outcome, and the risk of failure of the specific project or program is borne by the guarantor. As Mario Simonsen has said: "Loans to Itaipu are project loans only if Citibank is willing to take cruzeiros or electric power."

This nonspecific nature of bank credit has two effects. First, it means that risks inherent in projects or strategies are shifted to the lender only through nonperformance at the country level. This costly and inefficient mechanism results in very limited risk spreading. The predominance of general obligation financing, coupled with clauses prohibiting the pledging of specific revenues for the repayment of foreign obligations, is the result of a reaction to the experience of Latin American borrowers in the 1930s, whose external borrowings were secured by pledges of revenues (port authority receipts, customs duties, utilities charges, and so on) to the point that these countries had little room to maneuver, triggering defaults. Further, the resulting conflicts among creditors inhibited rescheduling of the loans in question.

There is little question that the shift to general obligations, coupled with negative pledge and pari passu clauses,[17] has resulted in greater financial flexibility for borrowers, as well as greater protection for and reduced conflict among lenders. This flexibility and confluence of interest of 100 principal lenders has been a major factor in the limitation of crises (through reschedulings). However, this benefit brings with it two costs. First, it extends public backing to all loans, whether or not the projects turn out to have been worthwhile, and thus precludes the shifting of risk to the foreign investor (except through nonperformance at the country level with its attendant costs). Second, it rules out earmarking the revenues of specific undertakings for debt service, and in that way may preclude the external financing of highly promising projects with the misfortune to be located in a country whose general creditworthiness is poor.

While general obligation financing is appropriate for financing countercyclical public expenditures or infrastructure projects that provide no direct financial return, its costs may often outweigh its benefits in the case of market-oriented, profit-seeking projects. Such financing for these projects exposes the public purse to miscalculation, mismanagement, and bad luck. By the same token, the use of general obligation finance removes these projects from the discipline of financial markets, thus shifting the full responsibility for project selection and management to the typically ill-equipped local government. It limits the role of private banks and public institutions in project evaluation to oversight of national economic strategies. Since all claims are general obligations of the sovereign, a loan to a good project is no better than a loan used to acquire arms or maintain consumption in the face of a reversal in the terms of trade.

The alternatives to general obligation finance include stand-alone finance, otherwise known as limited recourse project finance (i.e., loans that can be serviced only out of the revenues generated by the project), direct equity investment, and quasi-equity investments such as production shares or incentive contracts. Some of these alternatives, notably limited recourse project finance and production shares, may permit the reduction or elimination of transfer risk, where the foreign exchange or output generated by the project can be used directly to repay the foreign investor independently of the country's general situation. Note that the reduction in transfer risk may bring with it an increase in expropriation risk as well as commercial risk. In other cases the investor will remain subject to transfer risk.

---

17. A negative pledge clause prohibits the borrower from taking actions that might impair the lender's claim, such as pledging specific revenues to other lenders or giving other lenders senior rights in the case of rescheduling. A pari passu clause requires that all creditors be treated alike.

Under all these alternatives the financier will have a strong interest in assuring that the project or program being financed is well conceived and executed. Further, to the extent that industrial country interests control outcomes critical to a program or project's success, their acceptance of a stake will encourage them to seek to influence policies in ways that are favorable to the project. For example, an oil company with a production-sharing contract is less likely to support a levy on US oil imports than one receiving a fixed fee for managing a foreign oil field.

CONCENTRATION OF DEFAULT IMPACT

The fact that loans to developing countries are concentrated in commercial banks has magnified the potential impact of nonperformance on the system, and threatened the continued availability of finance for these countries. As of summer 1985, Morgan Guaranty has calculated that loans to all developing countries amounted to some 141 percent of the primary capital of US banks, down from a peak of 186 percent at the end of 1982.

When developing-country debt is viewed relative to the total value of financial claims outstanding in the world economy, though, it does not loom nearly as large. For example, as noted earlier, the total capitalization of major world markets exceeded $11.5 trillion in 1980, placing total developing-country obligations at well under 10 percent. While this percentage is by no means trivial, it does suggest that the world financial system could absorb the loss of a significant proportion of claims on developing countries if the effects of such a loss were spread throughout the system.

In order to assess the impact of a major default on the world financial system, it is useful to compare its potential magnitude with financial losses experienced in recent years. In the United States, during 1973 and 1974, share values fell by almost 40 percent, or roughly $600 billion, yet the system did not collapse.[18] Moreover, a major default could force banks to further limit lending or even to cease rolling over existing credits.

---

18. Even if the banking authorities of industrial countries were to intervene quickly to avert any run on banks that might result from a major default, the distributional impact of such a default would be quite different from that of an equivalent drop in equity values. The former would be covered primarily with an initial monetary expansion (a tax on money-fixed holdings) and a later requirement for higher general tax revenues, while the latter would involve a loss in savings for retirement, etc., which probably would have a smaller impact on output in industrial countries. Further, there is no guarantee that banking authorities would, in fact, intervene to avoid a collapse of any element of the system.

Appraisal of the Current Structure: Direct Foreign Investment

Direct investment, which has traditionally been the most important mechanism for providing risk capital, is motivated by the return that the parent expects to be able to earn by linking a local facility with its existing network of production or marketing operations. Typically, such investment is most attractive when the firm can carry over to other locations expertise (for example, regarding technology or marketing) that it is already exploiting elsewhere, or when costs differ sufficiently by location to justify shifting certain activities offshore.

As a result of these features, the level and composition of direct investment are in large part determined by factors specific to particular industries or firms. It has in practice tended to be concentrated in a few countries with attractive domestic markets, primary production possibilities, or export opportunities. The resulting level of capital flows need not correspond to the macroeconomic need for a capital inflow. On the other hand, there is a significant tendency for profits, and therefore profit remittances, to decline in periods of domestic recession. When a recession is the result of payments difficulties, this feedback can be quite helpful: for example, according to IMF data, debits for direct investment income in the indebted developing countries fell from a peak of $15.0 billion in 1981 to $12.0 billion in 1983.

In addition to shifting a part of the macroeconomic risk to foreign investors, direct investment gives the investing firm an incentive to provide appropriate forms of intangible capital, and a direct stake in the performance of the local venture. These factors are of critical importance where intangible capital is involved, since under these circumstances it is difficult to specify performance standards or to evaluate responsibility when they are not met.

As noted earlier, direct investment in developing countries has traditionally been of two types: *resource-seeking investment,* which seeks to exploit comparatively abundant local raw materials; and *market-seeking investment,* which seeks to exploit local market opportunities for goods produced locally but employing experience gained elsewhere. In recent years, though, an increasing proportion of direct investment has been what is termed *efficiency-seeking investment,* which seeks to exploit comparative advantages in particular stages of production. While this began with offshore assembly in Asian countries with relatively low labor costs, it has been extended both geographically and in terms of the activities involved. For example, firms have located engineering and software activities in India to exploit its low-cost pool of professionals, while the production of electronic components has followed assembly to Asian countries that are developing a higher skill level. Meanwhile, some of the traditional low labor cost operations have sought new locations, including the US-Mexican border.

In an increasing number of cases, market-seeking and efficiency-seeking investments are being combined. This occurs where access to local markets is granted in return for performance requirements involving a commitment to produce output for sale on a global scale, part of which is sold locally while the rest is "exchanged" for complementary imports. Such offset schemes are particularly prevalent in Brazil and Mexico.[19]

One of the major effects of the debt crisis has been the realignment of the commercial and financial policies of indebted countries. The change is most marked in Latin America, where overvalued real exchange rates have been eliminated by major real devaluations. One result has been to increase the opportunities for export-oriented investment in general, and particularly for efficiency-seeking direct investment. A number of countries, including India and the members of the Andean Group, have also reoriented their policies in recent years with a view to increasing the influx of direct investment.

In terms of the desired attributes of external finance, direct investment very closely matches foreign-exchange remittances to the local operation's capacity to pay and, to the extent that these profits are subject to the same risk factors as the economy as a whole, it also provides a reasonable match with the country's capacity to remit foreign exchange. Since it provides foreign investors with a direct stake in the success of the local undertakings, it also has favorable incentive effects from the viewpoint of the host society. These, however, may be weakened somewhat because of the conflicts of interest that often occur between the multinational firm seeking to maximize its global financial profits and the host society with its interest in maximizing local value-added. This is especially true in countries with substantial price distortions relative to the world economy.

The credibility of direct investment as a financial contract depends on the ability of the investing firm to withhold critical inputs or valuable access to its sourcing and product networks, as well as on the sanctions that can be imposed by investor governments in case of expropriation or other policy measures that reduce the value of the foreign investor's claim. As these sources of leverage have declined in many industries, direct investment has been subject to increasingly stringent controls and requirements to the extent

---

19. For a discussion of investment incentives and performance requirements, including such production offsets, see Guisinger et al. (1985).

that, in at least some countries and industries (notably extractive industries), it is no longer attractive to foreign investors.[20]

The major limitations of direct foreign investment stem from the same characteristics that provide its principal distinctive advantage—the penetration of the host economy by a foreign firm and its open-ended nature. This penetration is beneficial to the host country to the extent that it provides a greater flow of technology, better incentives, or increased access to firms' international sourcing and sales networks than would otherwise be possible. However, it is detrimental to the host society to the extent that this foreign control over domestic economic activities subjects it to abuses of market power, imposes undesired values on it, or reduces the scope for domestic institutional development. Since direct investment to a considerable extent substitutes foreign managerial and financing mechanisms for domestic ones, it is often viewed by critics as hampering domestic development in these regards. Its proponents, however, argue that it enhances this development through the transfer of organization models and the development of local managerial and financial talent.

From a contracting perspective, the open-ended nature of direct investment implies that the investor is subject to a wide range of risks. These include commercial risks, expropriation risks, transfer risks, and the risk of changes in commercial policies. Given this contractual complexity, mechanisms that allow the unbundling of various risks, such as the investment guarantees provided by OPIC or potentially the commercial insurance of transfer risk, can play an important role. For the same reasons, MIGA might be expected to increase the flow of direct investment. However, there should be no illusions that direct foreign investment will return to its earlier importance and provide a major proportion of developing countries' financing needs. Its primary function is to provide risk capital in conjunction with other tangible and intangible inputs in those cases where the linkage of local activities with those of a foreign firm is economically desirable and where the resulting degree of foreign control is acceptable.

---

20. This situation of declining investor leverage prevalent in extractive industries is known as the "obsolescing bargain." In the case of existing projects, it almost inevitably leads to a deterioration of the foreign investor's claim. In a dynamic setting, though, if potential investors see that contracts will rapidly become obsolescent, they will cease to make further investments.

4 Financial Instruments

If international capital mobility is in the future to realize its considerable potential for economic good, it will be necessary both to broaden the sources of finance and to improve its terms so as to achieve a better distribution of risks and rewards. Prompt action to those ends should also help to alleviate, if only marginally, the foreign-exchange stringency that is likely to afflict many developing countries for several years yet as they struggle to emerge from the debt crisis. General obligation borrowing, including but not limited to floating-rate bank credit, will continue to be a desirable component of all countries' mix of international finance. In fact, given the circumstances in the banking sector, the challenge will be to find ways to maintain a reasonable volume of such flows.

The present section analyzes a number of financial mechanisms, several of which would represent innovations, that might be able to augment the flow and improve the structure of the external borrowing of developing countries. The mechanisms are grouped under three headings:

- those involving a flow of risk capital

- those providing credit flows that do not involve general obligations—"stand-alone" finance

- those that might broaden the sources or improve the terms of general obligation finance.

The standards we use to appraise those mechanisms are those developed in the previous section: whether they diversify the sources and types of financing arrangements to assure greater continuity, reduce risks and transfer those that remain to those parties most able to bear them, improve the matching of obligations with ability to pay both in terms of hedging and time matching, and maintain or improve the flexibility of terms.

Risk Capital

All investment involves risk taking. However, when a developing country finances an investment project by incurring debt, it implicitly accepts virtually all of the risks of the activity being financed. Losses can be passed on to the lender only by default or the credible threat of default—a very costly strategy for the borrower as well as the lender. As a corollary, the lender has little stake in the success of the project, and hence has little motivation for intervening in its design or management.

At the national level, reliance on conventional forms of debt as the source of foreign capital increases the variability of foreign-exchange revenues net of debt-service requirements, relative to the variability of the foreign-exchange flows generated by the underlying real activities. This implies an increased variability in import capacity, which in turn tends to increase the magnitude of fluctuations of domestic absorption and may limit the country's ability to borrow abroad.

In addition to direct foreign investment, the two primary mechanisms that do involve a transfer of risk from borrower to lender are portfolio investment in equities and what may be termed quasi-equity investments, where the lender is entitled to an income stream that depends in a well-defined way on the success of the project but with a narrow claim to participate in ownership or control.

Each of these mechanisms has drawbacks as well as advantages. Different mechanisms will accordingly be called for in different contexts, and the most appropriate mix will vary from one country to another. The following discussion seeks to identify these advantages and disadvantages, with a view to providing a basis for evaluating the role that the various mechanisms might play.

PORTFOLIO INVESTMENT IN EQUITIES

A major potential source of risk capital is portfolio investment in stocks (equities) quoted on public stock markets. Like the direct investor, the equity investor seeks a share in the profits of private enterprise. Unlike the direct investor, however, the equity investor is seeking *only* a share of profits, and not the responsibilities of control. Indeed, most equity investors deliberately restrict their holdings to a small percentage of the total stock (less than 5 percent), with a view to avoiding any difficulty of selling out and any danger of being forced into taking responsibility for saving the firm if they lose confidence in its management.

There has in recent years been a sharp increase in cross-border equity investment among the OECD countries, particularly on the part of pension funds, which are by far the largest institutional purchasers of equities. Foreign commitments of US pension funds reached $16 billion at the end of 1984, more than double their level only two years earlier. By the end of 1982 British pension funds had placed some 15 percent of their assets abroad, a proportion that had risen from only 6 percent three years earlier when exchange controls were abolished (Nowakowski 1983). The proportion has risen further since, perhaps to as much as 25 percent. Similarly, the liberalization of capital outflows by Japan allowed Japanese pension funds to use up to 20 percent of the monthly increase in their portfolios to acquire foreign assets up to 10 percent of their portfolios; by March 1985 they had placed about 8.3 percent of their total assets abroad. Nowakowski estimated that at the end of 1982 some 4 percent of the worldwide assets of private pension funds, or $43 billion out of a world total of $1,175 billion, was invested outside the home market. Both the total portfolio and the proportion held in foreign assets are by now substantially larger, and growing rapidly.

A second source of institutional demand for foreign equities comes from the life insurance companies. However, despite the substantial assets (over $700 billion in the United States) managed by these companies, the sums involved here are much smaller, in part because insurance companies still invest primarily in bonds, and possibly also in part because at least in the United States they are much more heavily regulated. In New York, which is critical because companies need to comply with its regulations in order to do business there, insurance companies are forbidden to hold more than 1 percent of their assets abroad (plus up to 10 percent in Canadian securities).[21] Companies with foreign subsidiaries are also allowed to hold assets in those countries to match their liabilities there, and a "basket clause" permits an additional 5 percent of the portfolio to be invested in any form, including foreign assets—though it has rarely been used for that purpose. Other states have broadly similar regulations.

Japanese insurance companies face limits similar to those of pension funds; as of March 1985 the top nine life insurance funds had placed 9.1 percent of their portfolio abroad. British companies may be restrained by a regulation that only stocks quoted on a stock exchange approved by the Department of Trade can be bought for investment-linked life policies. It so happens that the only exchanges in what the IMF classifies as developing countries that have received approval are those in Brazil, Hong Kong, Johannesburg, Kuala Lumpur, Mexico, and Singapore.

The reasons for the increase in international equity investment are not hard to find. The most important is the rapid acceptance of the theory of risk diversification that emerged out of academic work in the 1960s: it is now well understood that the overall risk of a portfolio can be reduced, and its expected return increased, by holding a widely diversified portfolio, even if

---

21. New York Insurance Law 81-a.1(g) of September 18, 1983.

some of the securities in it are individually quite risky. Not only has this been accepted intellectually by the financial community, but in 1974 it was embodied in the Employee Retirement and Income Security Act (ERISA). This legislation provides the basis for regulation of US pension funds; it explicitly accepted that pension fund managers could satisfy their fiduciary responsibility for prudent management of the sums entrusted to them by appropriate diversification, provided that they undertake the research needed to satisfy themselves that securities offer an expected return commensurate with their risk characteristics. Moreover, the theory has been confirmed by experience; for example, American investors who had already diversified internationally before the late 1970s found that their foreign holdings provided valuable support to overall returns during the period of a weak dollar. A second factor supporting increased international equity investment is the marked improvement in information on foreign companies—a product of the information revolution. And of course a third factor is that the sums available— particularly in pension funds—have been growing rapidly, in most cases faster than the capitalization of the domestic equity market.

Up to now the vast majority of international equity investment has taken place *among* the developed countries. Well over 90 percent of the foreign investments of US pension funds are placed in other OECD countries. In fact, foreign equity investment in what the IMF classifies as developing countries has been of significant size in only five countries (Hong Kong, Israel, Malaysia, Singapore, and South Africa), of which only Malaysia would be classified unambiguously as a developing country. Hong Kong, Singapore, and South Africa probably account for over 90 percent of such foreign investments as US pension funds have made outside the OECD. Total foreign equity investment in the ''core'' developing countries listed in table 6 has been estimated at $700 million, with a further $50 million invested by institutions and the general public in a few developing-country stocks listed on developed country stock exchanges (van Agtmael 1985).

The bulk of such investments as have been made by foreign investors in developing-country equities has taken place through the medium of investment funds. Thus, $150 million has been invested in Mexico through the Mexico Fund, $120 million in Korea through two funds, some $50 million each through several funds in Taiwan and Brazil, and $50 million in India (in a fund accessible only to Indian expatriates). A Thai Fund has just been set up by Merrill Lynch in association with the International Finance Corporation (IFC). Perhaps another $100 million has been invested through regional funds in Southeast Asia.

Some of these funds are closed-end mutual funds (unit trusts, in British terminology), which raise an initial sum of money from the public and other

T A B L E 6   **Market capitalization of equity markets in developing countries, 1980 and 1983 (billion dollars)**

Country	1980	1983	Net bank debt, 1983
Malaysia	12.4	22.7	4.6
Brazil (São Paulo)	13.0ᵃ	13.1	56.4
Taiwan	6.1	8.7	3.4
India	6.0	8.0	−1.5
Israel	4.8	5.1	−2.8
Korea	3.8	4.0	21.6
Mexico	13.0	3.0	51.8
Chile	10.3	3.0	8.6
Jordan	1.6	2.9	−1.2
Venezuela	2.7	2.7ᵃ	13.4
Thailand	1.2	1.5	3.7
Argentina	4.0	1.4	19.3
Pakistan	0.7	1.2ᵃ	−1.2
Colombia	1.6	1.0	3.7
Philippines	1.9	0.7ᵃ	10.0
Zimbabwe	1.8	0.3	0.9
Indonesia	0.1	0.3	4.4
Kenya	0.5	0.2	−0.4
Total	85.5	79.8	194.7
Memorandum items			
Hong Kong and Singapore	65.2	58.3	16.2
South Africa	100.0	82.8	14.9
United States	1,238.0	1,641.7	n.a.
World	2,518.9	3,116.2	n.a.

n.a. Not applicable.
Note: Data are year-end values in terms of billions of US dollars, converted at official exchange rates, of the market capitalization of domestic companies quoted on stock exchanges. (The Singapore figure includes international, predominantly Malaysian, companies.) Market capitalization has not been consolidated per country in case of more than one stock exchange.
Source: Van Agtmael, *Emerging Securities Markets,* exhibit 2.8. For bank debt, BIS 1984.
a. Estimate.

financial institutions which they invest in the securities of a particular market (or set of markets). The portfolio is actively managed, while the shares of the investment fund are simultaneously traded on one of the major world securities markets, usually New York or London. This arrangement enables an individual investor to withdraw from a particular developing country without requiring that country to supply foreign exchange, since his holding is bought by another foreign investor: the country needs to provide foreign exchange only for dividend remittances. The main disadvantage of closed-end funds is that they require considerable scale to achieve the critical mass of investors that will provide liquidity on a secondary market.

The alternative is an open-end mutual fund, where the manager of the fund stands ready to buy or sell stocks in the local market in response to net deposits or withdrawals in the fund by investors. This is practical only in countries with fairly liquid securities markets and without exchange controls, and has the disadvantage to the host country of subjecting it to foreign exchange losses whenever foreign investors seek a net withdrawal of their funds. On the other hand, open-end funds can operate on a smaller scale. Investors pay or receive the current market value of the stocks in the fund (plus or minus a margin to cover costs). Semi-open-end funds are open-end funds that become closed-end in response to prespecified contingencies like exchange control: a number of the smaller funds take this form, and are in consequence usually limited to institutional investors.

That past equity investment has been limited does not imply that the potential for *future* equity investment is similarly limited. Table 6 shows that market capitalization of equities in developing countries was quite substantial at the end of 1983, and in most cases it has risen greatly since. Even excluding the "marginal" developing countries of Hong Kong, Singapore, and South Africa, market capitalization was some $80 billion at the end of 1983 (and rises to $221 billion if the marginal cases are included). This is modest compared to total world market capitalization of over $3 trillion (although it was about 25 percent of the capitalization of European markets), or compared to the $218 billion bank debt at the end of 1983 of the 18 listed countries (all those with significant active securities markets). But it is large enough to provide the basis for meaningful capital inflows in the future.

Suppose, for example, that foreign investors were to try over time to acquire the same proportion of the value of developing-country equities that they have of the equities of OECD countries other than their own. That proportion may now be on the order of 5 percent. If capitalization remained constant at the end-1983 level, that would mean they would be seeking to build up a holding equal to some $4 billion, over five times their present assets. If such a shift were spread out over three or four years, one would see capital inflows of over $1 billion a year. But of course market capitalization does not remain constant. On the contrary, as shown in table 7, the capitalization of most markets increased dramatically during the 1970s, even measured in dollars. Admittedly, capitalization tended to stagnate from 1980 to 1983 (table 6), but this was a consequence of the debt crisis and is unlikely to persist in the future. If capitalization were to grow at 20 percent a year

TABLE 7 **Growth of capitalized value of certain equity markets during the 1970s (percentage)**

	Cumulative growth	Average annual growth
Argentina, 1966–80	425	13
Chile, 1963–80	5,738	27
Hong Kong, 1972–80	172	13
Jordan, 1978–80	193	71
Korea, 1969–80	1,248	27
Mexico, 1966–80	1,341	21
Singapore, 1969–80	2,335	34
Thailand, 1976–80	279	40

Source: Van Agtmael, *Emerging Securities Markets,* exhibit 2.4.

on average, which appears far from unreasonable in the light of table 7, total market capitalization would reach $138 billion in 1987, and the *increase* in capitalization that year would be some $28 billion. Foreign purchases of just 5 percent of this *increase* would yield a capital inflow of almost $1.5 billion. Even this may underestimate the potential: an inflow of foreign money would tend to raise stock prices and lower the cost of equity capital to private firms in developing countries, thus increasing market growth both through larger capital gains and through encouraging new issues. Thus, while the inflows will certainly not come close to matching the cutback in bank lending, there is scope for capital inflows of a useful size through the medium of equity investment.

Is it conceivable that investors in the industrial countries could develop a taste for such investments? The same reasons that were invoked above to explain the rapid growth of intra-OECD international equity investment suggest that it is possible that these flows will in the future increasingly spill over to the equity markets of developing countries if this is permitted by the host countries. In the first place, returns tend to be high: the average shown in table 8 was 25 percent a year from 1976 to 1983, as against the world average of 12 percent. Second, returns have (at least in the late 1970s) shown a low correlation with those in the major developed countries (even lower than those among the developed countries), thus making these assets an attractive medium for portfolio diversification (van Agtmael 1984, exhibit 2.29). Third, information on these markets is improving, nurtured by the IFC. Finally, the funds seeking investment are still growing rapidly, and will go on doing so.

There are a number of common misgivings about investing in these markets, most of which have a basis of truth in at least some markets, but none of

T A B L E 8   **Return on investment in emerging markets, 1976–83 (percentage)**

Country group	1976	1977	1978	1979	1980
Emerging markets					
Argentina	147.0	−43.6	79.9	233.6	−72.2
Brazil	1.3	11.9	−6.0	−12.5	4.1
Chile	103.4	146.3	56.3	131.6	92.7
Hong Kong	40.0	−11.0	18.0	80.0	71.0
India	34.1	13.7	51.2	21.1	42.3
Jordan[c]	—	—	53.4	27.7	21.5
Korea	72.4	114.2	23.7	−13.0	−26.5
Mexico	19.1	22.3	127.8	96.3	17.7
Singapore	14.0	6.0	52.0	−12.0	29.0
Thailand	0.4	187.7	43.2	−40.7	−12.9
Zimbabwe	13.2	3.1	−6.9	178.7	30.4
Industrial countries					
United States	23	−8	6	14	29
Japan	25	15	52	−12	29
Cumulative return					
Capital International world index[e]	114	116	136	152	192
IFC emerging market index[f]	134	196	304	514	645

Note: The returns depicted are calculated as follows. Assume a US investor has $100 to invest in an emerging market. After conversion to domestic currency, the proceeds are placed in a basket of actively traded stocks. Dividends may be paid on the investment during the year, and capital gains may also be secured if the market price of the stock rises. These two sources of income are converted back to US dollars at year-end exchange rates to yield a return denominated in US dollars. This return is expressed as a percentage of the original $100 investment.

Source: World Bank 1985, table 9.2.

a. Returns for 1983 are up to the end of November for Argentina and to the end of December for Brazil, Hong Kong, India, Jordan, Mexico, Singapore, Thailand, and Zimbabwe.

b. Based on preliminary data for 1983.

c. Jordan's stock market opened in January 1978, hence data are not available for earlier years.

d. Based on *Capital International* data for 1981–83, including net dividends.

e. Based on *Capital International* data; January 1, 1976 = 100.

f. Returns in emerging markets included in this table, except for Hong Kong and Singapore, on a market-weighted basis (1980 for 1975–80; individual years for 1981–83); January 1, 1976 = 100.

1981	1982	1983[a]	Average annual change 1976–83[a]
−54.5	66.2	124.5	18.7
9.0	−19.9	97.4[b]	6.6[b]
−48.3	−52.1	−18.4	27.7
−16.0	−42.0	−8.6	9.2
23.8	−5.9	6.0	22.0
35.0	8.0	−7.0	19.9
40.2	7.9	7.4	21.5
−46.8[d]	−79.8[d]	170.2[d]	−0.6[d]
15.0	−1.0	29.2	15.0
−19.2	21.1	9.7	12.3
−56.7	−32.4	−7.9	0.8
−4	21	20	13.5
15	−1	23	16.8
184	205	250	12.1
593	412	617	25.5

which appears sufficient to justify ruling out careful investment. For example, although the private sector is in most cases smaller than in industrial countries and a number of the privately owned companies are often closely controlled, most markets have some stocks of large corporations that are sufficiently actively traded to offer investors liquidity. Accounting, auditing, and disclosure standards rarely match those in the Anglo-Saxon world, but they are improving and are now in many cases comparable to those in continental Europe. Devaluation is normally compensated in due course by high appreciation of the stock in terms of local currency. Withholding taxes on dividends, and capital gains taxes, are an obstacle in many but not all countries. Insider trading is no worse a problem than in other markets outside the United States, United Kingdom, and Canada. Exchange controls (and the fear of their future introduction or tightening) undoubtedly constitute a deterrent to investment in some countries, but in a number the regulations are quite liberal (or even nonexistent).

The attitudes of institutional asset managers toward investing in developing-country equities are varied in the extreme. It is not difficult to find managers who express relief at having avoided buying themselves a packet of trouble like the banks. But it is also possible to find those who are convinced that the rewards of discriminating investment in these markets amply outweigh the trouble and risks. In between are those who would not dream of putting a major share of their portfolio into these markets, but are quite open to the possibility of placing 1 percent or 2 percent there, in the same way that they regard it as reasonable to place a small proportion of their portfolio in venture capital stocks with high risks but the possibility of exceptionally high returns. There is enough open-mindedness overall to sustain the possibility of significantly larger flows than have occurred in the past, if the host countries relax the restrictive attitudes that have deterred inflows up to now.

Although developed countries place certain obstacles which may discourage a flow of equity finance to the developing countries, as noted in the next section, the main impediments arise from the side of the host countries. A few markets, notably those of Hong Kong, Malaysia, and Singapore, are completely open to foreign investment. Those in Chile, Israel, Jordan, the Philippines, and Thailand are also relatively free (although withholding taxes are substantial in the latter two cases). Brazil, Korea, and Taiwan limit foreign investment to special mutual funds; Mexico allows holdings of a few specified stocks in addition to the Mexico Fund. Argentina and Venezuela impose a minimum holding period requirement that acts as a significant deterrent to foreign investment. The markets of Colombia, Kenya, India,

Indonesia, Pakistan, and Zimbabwe are essentially closed to foreign investment.[22]

Is the restrictive attitude of so many countries to foreign equity investment sensible? It is not necessary to prevent local firms from coming under foreign control (a fear that should be respected whether or not it is endorsed). Legislation could perfectly well stipulate maximum limits to foreign share ownership (say 5 percent to any individual foreign holder, and 25 percent for foreigners in general), without impeding a major expansion in foreign equity holdings. Indeed, Korea is planning to liberalize foreign portfolio investment in the next few years, and is imposing such regulations (with a maximum of 10 percent on foreign holdings in any company). Even the United States requires notification of the Securities and Exchange Commission if an individual foreign holder acquires more than 5 percent.

An alternative and even more secure method of avoiding any danger of foreign control could be conceived. It would involve the issue of two distinct classes of shares, say "A" and "B." The A shares would constitute the majority and be available for holding only by domestic residents (or citizens). The B shares would be limited to (say) 25 percent of the total and would be available either to domestic residents or to foreigners. If desired, the B shares could even be without voting rights. Another possible twist is to make the A shares registered shares (to ensure that the residency requirement is satisfied) and the B shares bearer shares (to appeal to the desire for anonymity of some international investors). The only apparent drawback of this scheme is that it might provide a mechanism for capital flight (by buying B shares and selling them to foreign investors), but, since the capital outflow would necessarily be offset by an inflow, it would not be a disaster. In the absence of exchange controls or takeover battles, the B shares could go to a premium but not to a discount, and as long as they sold at a premium they would be exchanged just among foreigners and thus, like a closed-end fund, avoid any drain on the reserves.

Another possible objection is that equity investment is expensive. It is true that the total rate of return on equity investment, which averaged almost 26 percent a year from 1976 to 1983 (table 8), is in general higher than that on bank loans (which, at LIBOR plus 2 percent, cost an average of 12.7 percent from December 1975 to November 1983). But a substantial part of this return is in the form of capital gains and is therefore unlikely to represent a current

---

22. See van Agtmael (1984) for an extended discussion.

call on foreign exchange: indeed, if foreigners tried to withdraw funds on a large scale, the stocks would fall in value, discouraging such sales and reducing their cost to the economy. Furthermore, the distribution over time of debt-service payments would be less likely to cause problems, since both dividends and the market tend to fall at times (like the early 1980s) when countries face macroeconomic difficulties, and to rise at times of booming exports. But of course the central point is that it is worth paying a higher expected rate of return in order to pass on part of the risks to foreign investors.

The internal impact of an influx of foreign capital into equity shares would seem highly beneficial. The cost of capital to the private sector would fall, and its availability would rise, thus promoting expansion of a sector generally regarded as particularly valuable even by skeptics of the "magic of the market." This sector would also be able to reduce its dependence on loan capital, and thus its financial vulnerability to adverse shocks. Another advantage is that diversification of the sources of equity capital would be expected to provide the securities markets with an element of stability. It might be argued that a big influx of foreign capital would add to distributional inequities, by bidding up share prices and thus enriching existing shareholders, who are certainly not among the impoverished sector of the population in most countries. But, in a longer time perspective, higher equity prices are likely to be egalitarian rather than the reverse: local elites will no longer be able to gain such high rates of return from their savings.

It is to be expected that most equity investment will take the form of the purchase of quoted stocks. In addition, however, there are certain investors—of which the most conspicuous are venture capital funds—that aim to buy equity holdings through private placements in unlisted companies.

Venture capital funds have been established by a variety of financial institutions—banks, pension funds, insurance companies, investment trusts, and even the public sector. These funds are either allocated a small portion of the portfolio of their parent institution, or raise money from the public, including institutional investors. Their managers actively seek out promising new enterprises. They are normally not afraid of risk, where they see a possibility of a worthwhile return. While some restrict their investments to a limited geographical area, others have thought internationally from the very start. Indeed, British funds made many of their early investments in the United States, for lack of local capitalists planning promising ventures.

Some developing countries may be in a position to appeal to similar investment motives. While one does not expect them to be on the cutting edge of technological advance, they do not necessarily need to be: a developing country is, practically by definition, one where the application of established best-practice techniques is likely to be an innovative act. Moreover, a number of innovative opportunities specific to developing countries can be expected to open up in the next few years—like Amazonian fruits, intermediate technology, or the application of biotechnology to tropical agriculture. And an increasing number of developing countries have the entrepreneurial talent to give hope of exploiting the emerging opportunities.

While the sums of money likely to be yielded by equity investment (especially through private placements) are unlikely to be large in the short or even the medium run, there are clear advantages to removing the obstacles that have hitherto throttled this form of investment in most developing countries.

Investment in *real estate* is a rather straightforward way in which foreign investors are able to provide risk capital without requiring a great deal of management expertise or control over local operations. This is because of the unique nature of real estate investments, such as office buildings: once built and leased, they are more like passive portfolio investments than active direct investments. However, many countries prohibit or stringently control such investments. There seems no compelling reason for such a restrictive attitude: such investments may not yield benefits comparable to those of direct, equity, or quasi-equity investments in productive enterprises, but it is difficult to see that they pose any threat to the host country's objectives, and undoubtedly both institutional and private investors in the industrial countries would welcome the opportunity of investing in real estate in developing countries.

QUASI-EQUITY INVESTMENTS

It was argued in section 3 that a major weakness of the past organization of the international capital market was the concentration on lending instruments that were a general obligation of the borrower, with no tie to the outcome of the specific project for which funds were borrowed. Greater direct investment would be one antidote to this weakness, and greater equity investment, where the investor shares fully in the rewards and risks of a particular enterprise (though not in its control), would be another. But these are not the only alternatives that can be conceived.

An important recent development is an increasing tendency to "break open" the package deal that direct investment has typically constituted. Traditionally a single foreign-based firm would provide capital and technology and maintain control of its local subsidiary. In contrast, what have been termed the "new forms of international investment" (Oman 1984) involve joint ventures, licensing agreements, franchising, management contracts, turnkey contracts, production sharing, and international subcontracting. The attractions of these new forms of international investment are clear: they permit the host country to single out the particular features controlled by the foreign enterprise that cannot economically be obtained elsewhere, and to contract for those without allowing foreign control of the domestic operation. This unbundling has, in large part, been motivated by developing countries' desires to limit the degree of foreign penetration and control to those activities where access to foreign know-how or markets is most important. However, it can also serve to increase the flow of risk capital by allowing investors to limit their exposure to risks over which they have a comparative advantage by virtue of their diversification or expertise.

Instruments might be designed in several ways that would provide the investor with participation in certain risks (and hence potential rewards) without requiring the full set of preconditions necessary for equity investment. These may conveniently be referred to as quasi-equity instruments.

Examples of quasi-equity investments include production sharing, revenue sharing, or profit sharing through a variety of contract forms that may include contractual joint ventures, risk-service contracts, management or licensing agreements with incentive provisions and preference shares of various types. Some quasi-equities are variants on direct foreign investment in that they involve foreign firms that provide technology or access to markets, while others are akin to portfolio equity investment in that they involve arms-length investors with little ability to control project outcomes and little interest in doing so. Three such arrangements are discussed here: production sharing, revenue sharing, and profit sharing.

Different forms of quasi-equities might appeal to different groups of investors. Commercial banks specializing in project finance, pension funds, and insurance companies are likely to be candidates for arrangements that are, in effect, project loans with equity kickers. In contrast, quasi-equities that are akin to direct foreign investment in their requirements for technological or other know-how or their exposure to commercial risks can be expected to attract investments by multinationals.

Production Sharing

A production-sharing arrangement entitles the lender to a specified proportion of the output of a project in return for an input of capital and, perhaps, technology, marketing, and management skills. It is a form of foreign investment that has sometimes been employed in financing the development of mineral resources, as an alternative to direct investment, and this would indeed seem to be its natural role.

Direct investment in extractive industries fell out of favor with host countries because it was perceived (not without reason) as transferring the rents commanded by a country's natural resource endowment to foreign investors. The alternative that was generally adopted was nationalization associated with foreign borrowing, via bank credit, to finance development. This has also proved to be unsatisfactory, because it has greatly magnified balance of payments variability. Countries like Chile, Peru, and Zambia have overwhelming reasons to regret the form that the alternative to foreign ownership took.

Production sharing seems a natural intermediate solution that could satisfy the host country's desire to capture a large part of the rents generated by the exploitation of mineral resources without imposing on it excessive burdens when markets are weak.

Revenue Sharing

Under a production-sharing arrangement, the investor would claim title to a specified proportion of the physical production of the project. Under a revenue-sharing arrangement, his right would instead be to a specified proportion of the revenue generated by the project. It would be straightforward to draw up a revenue-sharing arrangement where a project's output is all exported, or where domestic sales are made at the world market price, but moral hazard inevitably arises where the price of domestic sales can be influenced by the local government. For example, the Carajas iron ore project in Amazonian Brazil would have been a good candidate for revenue sharing;[23] the Itaipu hydroelectric dam in Southern Brazil would not. It might be possible to safeguard against the danger of price manipulation by adopting a pricing formula, and using an MDB for surveillance to ensure that the contract is respected, although this could result in an undesirable loss of commercial flexibility—for example, precluding desirable price cuts if electricity was in unexpectedly abundant supply.

The main difference between a production-sharing and a revenue-sharing arrangement lies in who takes responsibility for determining the level of output and for sales. Production sharing creates the possibility of tension on

---

23. As it happens, Japanese and Italian investors in Carajas undertook to purchase a part of its output, an undertaking they are now seeking to shed in view of the world surplus of iron ore. Needless to say, this is a very different arrangement from the one commended in the text.

the former issue, whereas it is unambiguously the responsibility of the local firm under revenue sharing. Similarly, the local firm is responsible for selling the entire output, rather than only a part, under revenue sharing. Revenue sharing is therefore a suitable technique when the foreign investors wish to participate in the risks of the project but not in its control.

Profit Sharing

A profit-sharing arrangement goes one stage further than revenue sharing in giving the foreign investor a stake in the net (rather than the gross) outcome of the project, but without the share in ownership bestowed by an equity claim. By linking the stake to net outcomes, it provides the investor with incentives to control costs as well as to maximize revenues, but this typically also entails transferring to the foreign investor a degree of control over the operations in question. Further, since it involves various elements of domestic cost streams, and possibly domestic revenues, it is more sensitive to possible distortions in the pricing of these factor inputs and output.

The potential advantages of quasi-equity investments vis-à-vis more traditional equity forms are threefold. First, in most cases they expose investors to a narrower spectrum of risks, and thus permit further exploitation of comparative advantage in risk bearing when this advantage differs across categories of risks bundled together in traditional investments. Second, since they can be more explicit than equity contracts, they do not require as sophisticated a capitalist institutional infrastructure in the host country.[24] Third, since they generally expose investors only to certain relatively well-defined risks, they may be credible even when the investor has little or no control over the activity in question. Thus, they allow greater separation of ownership and control and, hence, limit foreign penetration of the host economy to activities where it is of mutual benefit.

To see these differences, consider alternative arrangements that may be used for financing the development of oil reserves in a developing country

---

24. By institutional infrastructure we refer to the myriad institutions and patterns of behavior that are required to sustain modern managerial capitalism with its separation of ownership and management and the widely dispersed nature of this ownership. These institutions include, inter alia, a tax system that minimizes the economic benefits of direct ownership of economic undertakings by individuals compared to ownership in the corporate form; corporate law and accounting that limit self-dealing by managers and define the rights of the various claimants under normal circumstances, as well as on recapitalization or liquidation; and securities market regulations that protect minority shareholders from insider trading and other forms of market manipulation.

(Blitzer, Lessard, and Paddock 1984). The key commercial risks in such an investment that must be borne by one party or another are the uncertainties regarding recoverable reserves, the price of oil in world markets, and the operating costs of the field. However, a number of risks involving the distribution of the gains between the two parties may make it difficult, if not impossible, to arrive at a mutually agreeable set of contract terms. Such risks include the obvious ones faced by the foreign producer of expropriation or some form of after-the-fact windfall profits taxes, but they also include risks faced by the host country in the form of reservoir stripping or, perhaps, underproduction, as well as a boycott of output in the event of a dispute. They also entail exposure of either party to general policy measures of the other (or, in the case of foreign investors, of their home country) that affect the profitability of oil production to the other. These risks include exchange controls and changes in general tax policies.

With traditional direct or portfolio equity investment, the foreign investor faces the whole spectrum of these risks. This will be inefficient if such investors do not possess a comparative advantage vis-à-vis the host country in bearing some of them, either because their exposures to such risks are greater or because the risks involve a substantial element of moral hazard, i.e., the possibility that the host government will influence outcomes to its benefit but to the detriment of the foreign investor. The degree of inefficiency, and hence the benefit of a more narrowly drawn risk contract, naturally depends on the specific circumstances of each investment.

With regard to the allocation of oil price risks inherent in the project that must be borne by one investor or the other, consider the contract a country with oil resources should seek with foreign investors. If it is a significant net exporter of oil, it will benefit from laying off some of its price exposure to world financial markets. Either equity or a production share would do this. Conversely, if it is a net importer, it will not want to pay an amount that varies significantly with the world price of oil, since this will reduce its benefit from having domestic production. It could do this with a contract that pays the foreign producer a fee per barrel of output that does not vary with the world price of oil.[25]

As an example of the allocation of risks involving moral hazard, consider again the case where a significant fraction of production is destined for the domestic market. A major risk that would be faced by direct or portfolio

---

25. To increase the credibility of such a contract, the fee could be on a sliding scale as a function of cumulative output, or the foreign investor's profits might be subject to an increasing "resource rent tax" as a function of cumulative profits.

investors in a domestic oil company is the pricing of the output in local markets. This pricing is a domestic policy choice and, as has been observed in both developed and developing countries, it is likely to be influenced by the degree of foreign ownership of the domestic oil industry. As a result, foreign investors would be unlikely to get involved unless they feel that they can exercise considerable control over domestic policy choices, yet such control is likely to be considered inappropriate meddling from the host country perspective. A risk-service contract[26] tied to world prices would avoid imposing this risk on the foreign investor, yet would expose the investor to the operating risks over which it does have significant control. Despite these benefits of unbundling various risks, investors in quasi-equities will remain subject to transfer risk, which may be a major deterrent to investors who would be willing to take certain commercial risks but not country exposure.

The potential magnitude of quasi-equity flows is large, as illustrated by the experience of one developing country that has used quasi-equity instruments on a big scale—Indonesia. Virtually all of its oil and gas development has been financed with production shares that provide foreign investors with 15 percent of output. These firms' profits arising from the production shares are also subject to Indonesian income tax, an efficient arrangement from Indonesia's perspective since these taxes are largely eligible for credit against firms' US tax liabilities. A rough estimate of the present value of these production shares held by foreign firms (predominantly oil companies) is $7.5 billion.[27] This compares to Indonesia's foreign indebtedness of $4.4 billion, and implies that by selling an additional 10 percent of its projected oil revenues, Indonesia could retire its general obligation financing.

As in the case of equity investment, many of the obstacles to increased quasi-equity flows lie in the policies of the developing countries themselves.

---

26. A risk-service contract typically has been defined as one in which the contractor is paid some multiple of the costs it has incurred *if* a commercial field is discovered. However, the concept can also be extended to a payment of a fixed fee per barrel or even a share of the value of the oil produced.

27. The present value is obtained by multiplying by five the value of the average annual foreign production share in the last three years. This calculation is based on the assumption that physical production of the fields under sharing contracts will decline exponentially at 10 percent a year, and that the appropriate real discount rate is 10 percent. Under these conditions, net present value equals (current flow)/$(k + e)$, where k is the discount rate and e is the exponential decline rate.

However, because of their novelty, these investments are likely to involve long gestation periods and require the gradual building of a successful track record to attract substantial sums. At the host country level, it appears that quasi-equity instruments have been spurned to some extent because of the high perceived cost of the upside participation obtained by the foreign investor. These same countries appear to have underestimated the cost of the downside risks they have retained by financing projects with general obligation borrowing.

Tax laws and foreign investment insurance schemes in investor countries have continued to favor direct investment over more limited forms of contractual involvement, although OPIC and several of the European insurance schemes extend to contractual schemes that do not involve ownership.[28] The World Bank confines itself exclusively to lending rather than taking risk positions, although the IFC has been involved in a number of interesting and innovative quasi-equity investments involving mining and forest-products firms. Because of the IFC's mandate to finance only private sector undertakings, however, these deals have typically been small. Since most large undertakings involve governments as parties, they have been excluded from such contracts.

While some industrial country governments, especially the United States, would prefer to see this problem disappear by shifting all such activities to the private sector, many countries do not meet the preconditions for successful private sector undertakings of this magnitude, or are unwilling to move so far. Rather than insist on private ownership, we believe that it is more important that such projects be undertaken on a stand-alone basis, even if the host government is a major party. The IFC has taken some initial steps in this direction, such as its participation in a Chinese joint venture with Peugeot. Such financing not only subjects these projects to the discipline of financial markets, but it protects the country from costs beyond its initial investment in the project.

One way to promote quasi-equity investments by portfolio investors might be to extend the World Bank's cofinancing program to cover such operations. The Bank itself could extend a government-guaranteed A-loan to cover part of the infrastructure investment associated with the project, while pension funds, insurance companies, or other investors bought (for example) claims

---

28. See Bergsten, Horst, and Moran (1978, pp. 163–64) for an early discussion of how US tax laws could be changed to be more even-handed between direct and non- (or quasi-) equity forms of investment.

that entitled them to a specified share of the revenues generated by the project. The World Bank would undertake to draw up the contract, aiming to avoid moral hazard. It would also take it upon itself to ensure that the terms of the contract were interpreted objectively and observed faithfully. Alternatively, the mandate of the IFC might be broadened to allow it to take quasi-equity positions in government-sponsored projects that could be structured on a commercial, stand-alone basis.

In addition, the World Bank (or another MDB) might assist risk unbundling by guaranteeing transfer risk (a much more limited guarantee than that currently provided under the Bank's B-loan guarantee option, see below). One modality might be to establish an account at the central bank which could back up one debt-service payment and be called if the central bank did not make foreign exchange available to the project entity. The government would then have to replenish this fund (or repay the MDB, if it was a guarantee that was called) within, say, 30 days. The MDB's position as a preferred creditor, as well as its disbursement pipeline, would (hopefully) ensure that the fund would always be "topped up" before the next debt-service payment date. Thus, the absence of a true risk-bearing capacity for the MDBs does not preclude them from playing a role in supporting quasi-equity investments. Rather, the nature of the MDBs' strengths, and their preferred creditor position, make them ideal for taking that part of the risk which can easily prevent such transactions from taking place, transfer risk.

Stand-Alone Finance

Another way to avoid some of the problems associated with general obligation finance is to link borrowings to particular enterprises or projects without a general guarantee. In such cases, the lender is exposed to the downside risks of the undertakings being financed, but in contrast to equity or quasi-equity claims, does not share in the upside potential. Clearly, therefore, the lender would require a higher expected interest rate on such loans than on general obligations, with the exception of cases where the commercial project risk is actually less than the country (transfer) risk and the lender can be shielded from the latter through the escrowing of export proceeds.

Such financing, sometimes referred to as project or limited recourse financing, links the return to the lender to the success of the project, but only up to the promised, contractual interest rate. Thus, the lender has a stake in the project's success, but only up to the level necessary to service the debt. From the perspective of the borrower, such financing may be thought of as borrowing at a rate that is independent of the project's success and purchasing insurance to service the debt in case the project fails. It may also involve the earmarking of project revenues for servicing the project borrowing.

Stand-alone finance has typically been employed by direct foreign investors in large extractive projects in order to limit their own downside risk and to exploit the banks' greater leverage over the governments of developing countries to increase the enforceability of their own claims.[29] For example, Occidental Petroleum recently announced a major investment in a Chinese coal project. Occidental's share of the investment is 25 percent, but 90 percent of this is borrowed from a consortium of banks on a stand-alone basis with no recourse to Occidental, implying that Occidental's equity stake is only 2.5 percent of the total investment. Since in such a case the lenders have no claim on the sponsoring firm, they have often turned to the host country where project revenues failed to cover debt service. In some cases, the lenders have obtained formal host-government guarantees. But even where they had no legal claim, they have sometimes brought pressure by arguing that default on a project financing would tarnish the host's reputation as an international borrower.[30]

To benefit from stand-alone finance, a developing country would need to achieve the type of provisions that multinationals have secured in the past, and to make unambiguously clear in advance that it accepts no responsibility for bailing out a failed project. The foreign investor would thus bear the commercial risk of the project's failure. In that event, the country is assured that implementation of the project will not result in a cash loss to the national economy. Peru would be in a materially better position today had it financed the trans-Andean pipeline on this basis in the 1970s, rather than on the basis of general obligation credit.

---

29. The now classic discussion of the use of project financing by Kennecott to increase the enforceability of its claims against Chile is provided by Moran (1973).

30. Several observers have noted that project loans in developed countries are riskier than loans on comparable projects in developing countries since default would tarnish the latter's overall reputation to a much greater extent than it would the former's. For example, contrast the reaction of financial markets to defaults in the United States of various real estate investment trusts (REITs) or Penn Central with the intense pressure brought to bear by foreign lenders on Mexico and Chile to make good on the obligations of local private firms, or on Indonesia to honor obligations entered into to pay for improperly contracted projects.

To persuade potential investors to accept the commercial risks of a project, however, it may be necessary to protect them against transfer risk. This can easily be achieved in the case of enclave export-oriented projects by escrowing the export proceeds. In some cases this might even enable a country to borrow on finer terms for a stand-alone project than would be possible for general obligations, despite the fact that the lender would be accepting the commercial risk of the project. The country would clearly gain through employing stand-alone finance where this was true.

The problem is that other creditors might lose. The principle of not pledging specific assets or revenues to strengthen general obligations rests on a sound basis. Such pledges provide the borrower with the worst of both worlds where the revenues of successful projects are encumbered and, hence, not fully available to the national treasury, while unsuccessful projects represent a drain on the treasury. To escrow substantial components of foreign-exchange earnings reduces a government's flexibility in difficult times and thereby prejudices the interests of other creditors.

While there are certainly circumstances where the other creditors can lose through the escrowing of export proceeds, there are also circumstances under which they would gain. Consider, for example, a country whose creditworthiness is too weak to sustain new general obligation borrowing, and which has a highly promising export-oriented project whose development would be impractical without foreign finance. A stand-alone project whose earnings were escrowed to cover debt service would permit the project to go ahead. At worst the country would have no more free foreign exchange than it otherwise would have had, leaving the position of existing creditors unaffected. But if the project was successful, it would add to the supply of free foreign exchange and thus benefit the position of the existing creditors.

Hence the financing of a market-oriented project on a stand-alone basis without recourse to the public purse may well provide sufficient additional benefits to warrant the pledging of a part of the additional revenue stream generated by the project. Enclave projects that generate direct export revenues, such as mines or oil fields, are in fact already sometimes financed on a limited recourse basis despite the preponderance of general obligation financing. This is possible by arranging to meet debt-service payments out of export proceeds before they are remitted to the host country. Such financing should be encouraged, provided that the reduction in transfer risk is limited to cases in which the lender accepts commercial risk.

Market-oriented projects that do not generate direct export revenues present a more complex problem. Even if financed on a limited recourse basis, they remain subject to transfer risk and, in many cases, to other risks emanating at least in part from domestic policy choices such as output pricing. These risks often inhibit financing from lenders who have the expertise to take on the commercial risks. As with quasi-equity investments, MDBs and investment guarantee authorities could do much to relieve this problem. An MDB, for example, might be able to introduce as project covenants the features and performance requirements that lenders need. Similarly, an MDB or a guarantee authority such as OPIC could provide guarantees against transfer risks. Such guarantees would be much narrower than those extended by the World Bank under its current B-loan guarantee program, and thus would allow greater specialization in risk taking.

General Obligation Finance

Important as is the underutilized potential of risk capital and stand-alone finance, there will always be a role for general obligation finance. This will be needed for any attempt to use foreign borrowing to smooth out shocks, since flows of risk capital and stand-alone finance are likely to vary with factors (notably the availability of promising projects) that bear no relation to the need for balance of payments finance. In view of our earlier argument that this factor makes it highly desirable to step up the flow of finance in the next few years, while the foreign-exchange constraint is binding, and the likelihood that any significant buildup in the flow of risk capital and stand-alone finance will take time, improving the volume and form of general obligation finance is a matter of some urgency.

This section starts by discussing the possibilities for better risk management through financial markets, either by the use of swaps or options or by selling assets whose return varies in a way that improves the match of debt service with ability to pay. A second subsection deals with instruments that might sustain and improve bank finance. The final part is concerned with the potentialities for increasing the role of the capital markets in providing suitable external finance to developing countries.

IMPROVED RISK MANAGEMENT

In recent years financial markets have developed novel techniques to allow agents to hedge some of the risks to which they are exposed, and the use of these techniques has been growing at an explosive pace. As yet, however, developing countries appear not to have exploited these opportunities. Further, although MDBs and particularly the World Bank have become quite active in using the techniques in the management of their own liabilities and liquid reserves, they have done little to exploit these instruments to match more closely the terms of their loans with the needs of developing-country borrowers.

The longest established markets of this nature are *futures markets* for commodities and *forward markets* for currencies. Futures markets could be used to lock in prices currently quoted as soon as reasonable estimates of crop size are available, thus permitting somewhat greater certainty that expenditures being planned for a few months ahead could be financed without drawing on the reserves. Similarly, the currency forward markets could be used to ensure that a known stream of export earnings denominated in one currency could be spent on goods whose price is denominated in another currency without a risk that subsequent exchange rate movements would force an unplanned drawdown of the reserves. In both cases, however, the opportunities for risk reduction are very limited, because the maximum maturities traded in these markets are short.

The new markets for *interest and currency swaps* appear to offer greater potential since the maturities offered are greater. An interest swap involves two parties, one of which typically has a fixed-interest obligation and the other a floating-interest obligation of similar size, agreeing to service each other's debt. The arrangement can be attractive to both parties where their preferences as to the form of debt they service do not match their comparative advantage in borrowing. For example, the World Bank is much better known in the bond markets than are most commercial banks, while both are about equally well placed to raise floating-rate debt. Hence both the World Bank and a commercial bank can gain, if the latter wishes to make a fixed-rate loan, by the World Bank's borrowing at a fixed rate and the two entering into a swap. The risk involved in entering a swap is limited but still significant, since a default by one's partner can oblige one to service the original loan standing in one's own name (while relieving one of the obligation to service the partner's loan).

Similarly, a currency swap typically involves two parties that have raised similar-sized loans denominated in different currencies agreeing to service each other's debts. This can be attractive to both parties where their projected foreign-exchange receipts arise in a currency that does not match their comparative advantage in borrowing different currencies. This could arise, for example, where a German corporation exports to the United Kingdom and thus has a net surplus of sterling earnings that can be used to service its borrowings, but is unknown to the UK capital market, while a British corporation is in the reverse situation (earning a deutschemark surplus but unfamiliar in Frankfurt). The risk involved in entering a currency swap is somewhat larger than that involved in an interest swap, given how sharply currencies can move and the fact that principal as well as interest obligations are swapped, although this is to some extent offset by the tendency of interest rates and exchange rates to move in opposite directions.

So far developing countries have made little use of the exploding swap markets. This may in part be due to a lack of interest on their part, arising from a failure to realize that currency swaps, in particular, offer the potential for a useful reduction in risk exposure. In fact, a significant contributory cause to the debt crisis was the reduction in the dollar value of developing-country exports induced by the dollar appreciation, which eroded the ability to service debts that were predominantly dollar-denominated. One way of avoiding this risk would have been to contract debts in a bundle of currencies that matched the destination of exports. A simpler technique now potentially available is to swap dollar debt-service liabilities for liabilities in a bundle of currencies that matches the currencies of price determination of the country's net exports.

Banks have so far been reluctant to enter into swaps with developing countries. They resist taking on a counterparty whose underlying liability could be rescheduled, and tend to demand prohibitive fees for such transactions. The recent emergence of a market for swap insurance may, however, enable developing countries to make significant use of this market in the future. Or an MDB could enter swaps in order to provide a particular borrower with a currency composition of debt-service obligations suited to its needs.

Another potential future development that might permit developing countries to improve their risk management would be further expansion of the *options* markets. Unlike a futures contract or a swap, an options contract does not oblige its purchaser to effect a future transaction at a price specified now, but simply gives the purchaser the right (i.e., option) of making such a purchase (or sale). Clearly he will decide to exercise his option and make that purchase (sale) only if the price specified in the option is lower (higher) than that prevailing when the option matures. The great potential advantage of options relative to forwards or swaps from the standpoint of developing-country borrowers is that the issuer accepts no exposure to the credit risk of the purchaser of the option, which is paid for in advance in cash. Thus, the existence of transfer risk should pose no barrier to use of this market.

At present both interest and currency options markets are too short term to provide any very useful protection to developing countries, but they are beginning to lengthen. Indeed, in recent months several borrowers, not yet including any developing countries, have been able to buy interest-rate caps in the options markets, for periods as long as 12 years. Bergsten, Cline, and Williamson (1985) urged the banks to make reimbursable interest-averaging caps (RIACs) available, for an appropriate charge, to developing-country borrowers. The emerging options market may enable the banks and MDBs to offer such facilities, or indeed an "absolute cap" with forgiveness of interest above the cap, and pass on the risk to others. The IDB, for example, could get greater mileage out of its interest-rate facility by applying the funds now used to give a straight interest subsidy to the purchase of options that would limit interest rates when they are highest. Alternatively, these markets may enable the borrowers themselves to purchase such insurance in the form of options contracts, while their contracts with their lenders remain in conventional floating-rate form.

With a sufficiently comprehensive and efficient set of options markets, indeed, a country might be able to achieve all the cash-flow matching that it wanted while still doing all its general obligation borrowing at floating interest rates. There are nevertheless two reasons why it might in fact benefit by borrowing in other forms. One is that options markets are still far from comprehensive and likely to remain so, however spectacular their future progress. For example, until there is an option on the price of copper 25 years in the future, Zambia may be able to gain protection by issuing 25-year bonds with a yield linked to the price of copper of a sort unattainable from the options markets. The other reason is that options markets may involve higher transaction costs than markets for the underlying assets. Even if a 25-year option on the copper price did exist, both potential lenders who wished to speculate or hedge on the price of copper and Zambia might be able to gain by Zambia's issuing bonds with a yield linked to the price of copper, rather than having both parties deal exclusively in options.

For those reasons we believe that it is still important to examine the possibility of creating financial instruments that would improve cash-flow matching. Besides commodity-linked bonds, like the copper-price-linked bonds mentioned above, these might include such instruments as index-linked bonds, constant-real-payment floating rate notes, and trade-linked bonds. We return to an analysis of these instruments below.

CONTINUED ACCESS TO BANK FINANCE

We have already suggested that a major challenge of the next few years will be to sustain an adequate flow of commercial bank lending to the developing countries: the total could even fall below the level of $15 billion a year projected in table 4.

Commercial and investment banks have in collaboration introduced in recent years a series of hybrid instruments—notably *note issuance facilities* (NIFs) and *revolving underwriting facilities* (RUFs). Their main purpose is to shift assets off the balance sheets of the commercial banks, and thus reduce their reserve needs, for a given level of credit extended to their customers, and thus for a given level of fee income generated. For example, a note issuance facility involves the sale of short-term notes backed with a guarantee by a group of underwriting investment banks to take up any unsold notes at each rollover date. The effect is therefore that of a medium-term loan commitment. A few of the most creditworthy developing countries (like Korea) have already exploited such facilities, which are significantly cheaper than standard Eurocurrency loans.

However, since the underwriters have a strong interest in not being left with unsaleable notes on their hands, they are bound to limit the availability of such facilities to the most creditworthy borrowers. Indeed, the regulators are starting to show concern for the risk that the underwriters may have to take on high-risk loans should the creditworthiness of the borrower be eroded during the life of the facility. Since April 1985 the Bank of England has required NIFs to be subject to capital adequacy requirements (to the extent of 50 percent of the face value of the facility). This will certainly reduce and might even eliminate the attraction of these instruments. Thus, at most these facilities offer a minor twist to those countries that retain voluntary access to the Eurocurrency market: it is quite mistaken to suppose that every innovation carries the promise of expanded access or better terms.

Proposals have been made in recent years to promote the establishment of a *secondary market in syndicated loans* (Guttentag and Herring 1985). These authors have suggested that the IMF (or some other agency) make a market by buying loans from the commercial banks that originate them, ensuring a degree of homogeneity by imposing eligibility requirements, pooling a number of loans to a given country, and selling off rights to shares in these pools. They point to the development of an efficient secondary market in mortgages by the Federal Home Loan Mortgage Corporation as a precedent for what can be achieved.

To some extent a secondary market exists already (Guttentag and Herring 1985, pp. 9–15), without either of the institutional developments that have been proposed to facilitate marketability. Although it is still thin, it appears to be developing rapidly. It primarily takes the form of swapping existing loans among banks that have a mutual interest in reallocating the country composition of their loan portfolios. Outright sales of existing loans appear to be less common and may involve distress pricing.[31]

Commercial banks have recently started introducing *transferable loan instruments* (TLIs), standardized contracts that facilitate the transfer of lending commitments from a primary lender to a secondary market. A TLI entitles its holder to receive all debt-service payments, as though the holder had been the primary lender, and leaves the obligations of the borrower unchanged. So far TLIs have been used only for industrial country loans, but they could be extended to developing countries.

Whatever the technique, there are long-run attractions in the development of a secondary market for bank loans, which would increase their liquidity and thus the willingness of banks to maintain or expand such lending. But there may also be short-run risks from the forced development of such a market. The American Institute of Certified Public Accountants (AICPA) has recently ruled that asset swaps are to be treated as the mutual sale of two loans, and that the "fair market value" of such loans must be established when a sale is made, with the loss from par absorbed in income. There is a presumption that the value of a loan to a country encountering debt-servicing difficulties is less than its face value. The same ruling notes that the price established in the sale/swap does not carry implications for the value of the remaining portfolio, i.e., that it need not be marked to market. Nevertheless, there remains some possibility that the regulators' requirements for capital adequacy might be influenced by the notional prices established for such transactions, and a fear of this possibility could increase the difficulty of securing continued collective action on the part of the banks.

The World Bank's *cofinancing program* is aimed at encouraging other lenders to participate in financing projects sponsored by the Bank. The cofinanciers may be commercial banks, export credit agencies, or official aid donors, with the banks being important in more creditworthy countries and aid donors offering concessional terms being the principal partners in low-income countries. The volume of export credits used in cofinancing World Bank projects has grown in recent years, and the Bank reports that "given

---

31. "The Market for Latin Debt," *New York Times*, 17 July 1985.

the constraints on official aid and the cautious approach of commercial banks to increasing their international exposure" it is now "pursuing a more systematic approach that would help borrowers secure export credits in larger volumes and possibly on better terms" (World Bank 1985, box 8.9).

Under its traditional form of cofinancing with the commercial banks, the World Bank and the private banks made separate and parallel loans to the same project, with or without an optional cross-default clause.[32] Where countries with cofinanced loans have rescheduled, these loans have been subject to rescheduling. Not surprisingly, this diminished the enthusiasm of the banks for engaging in cofinancing, so in 1983 the Bank introduced its program of B-loans, which provide for a much closer partnership between the two parties. This may take any one (or occasionally two) of three forms:

- direct lending, in which the World Bank participates in a syndicated loan, itself taking a share of the loan (on average about 12 percent, always concentrated in the longest maturities, thus generally guaranteeing that a default would involve the Bank)

- a guarantee option, under which the World Bank guarantees repayment of the longer maturities (typically 10 to 11 years) of a loan provided exclusively by the commercial banks

- contingency liability financing, which provides for level payments, after the grace period, so that if the interest rate rises above (falls below) a negotiated reference level the excess (deficiency) is deducted from (added to) principal due during the period and added to (deducted from) principal due at the end of the loan.

Cofinancing in 1983–85 has so far attracted about $2.5 billion in bank credits, leveraged by about $360 million of World Bank support. The program has been of greater importance than its size might imply, however, since it has been oriented particularly toward countries that might otherwise have been forced into rescheduling (certainly Hungary, conceivably Colombia), countries beginning to return to voluntary market access (Ivory Coast, perhaps Yugoslavia), and most recently to lubricate an involuntary new-money package (Chile). It is clearly playing a worthwhile role in extending the range of countries with access to bank finance, despite start-up difficulties and a lack of interest on the part of the more creditworthy borrowers (which presumably

---

32. That is, the clause gave the commercial banks the option of calling a default if the World Bank did so.

fear that cofinancing might limit their freedom to borrow from the commercial banks independently of World Bank approval). It is to be hoped that the present pilot program will be renewed in expanded form following the World Bank's forthcoming review.

The Inter-American Development Bank (IDB) has a broadly similar program, although technically it involves the sale of loan participations. Under these participations, the borrower continues to pay debt service to the IDB, while the IDB passes on money received to the bank that purchased the participation. Thus, the IDB does not carry the loan on its books, or any risk from the loan, and its capital is freed to undertake other investments. But the borrowing country retains its obligation to service debt to the IDB, and the loan retains its immunity from rescheduling. These two factors substantially reduce the risks confronting a commercial bank in purchasing a participation as opposed to extending a new credit, and hence expand the range of countries whose liabilities can be successfully marketed. On the negative side, the immunity from rescheduling would reduce the scope for after-the-fact flexibility that this mechanism provided during the debt crisis, which could aggravate any similar future difficulties, especially if the proportion of preferred creditors had risen substantially. Furthermore, this approach does little to familiarize the market with marginal borrowers, because there is no direct connection between the banks and the borrower.

The World Bank also used to have a program for selling off some of its loans as *sub-participations,* and this is being revived on a pilot basis. This program is essentially intended to liquify a portion of the outstanding portfolio of the World Bank's loans, some made as long as 15 years ago to then-developing countries like Japan! The main purpose is to provide headroom to enable the Bank to continue lending until it obtains another general capital increase (a topic discussed in the next chapter). By selling loans to large borrowers like India that are already near the self-imposed limit of 10 percent of its portfolio, the Bank also frees itself to make fresh loans. This program has much the same disadvantages as those of the IDB program: while some additional lending may be induced, this is at the cost of a reduction in the proportion of outstanding debt that could be rescheduled should the need arise.

In sum, the scope for stimulating the flow of bank loans seems distinctly limited. In the short run, something can be done by offering new lenders preferred creditor status through cofinancing or loan participations. It may be worth accepting the disadvantage of reduced long-run flexibility that this entails to start a country moving back toward voluntary borrowing, provided that its scale does not get out of hand. In the longer run, a secondary market may help reestablish the attractiveness of lending. The only other potential development that would seem able to stimulate the flow of bank lending would be the emergence of an active market for country-risk insurance, which would permit the banks to pass on the increase in sovereign risk to the insurance industry. A year ago there were hopes that such a market was emerging, when the news spread of a deal between Citibank and a consortium headed by CIGNA, but that deal fell through and the prospects for a growth in the private insurance of transfer risk do not currently appear bright (Bergsten, Cline, and Williamson 1985, option 5).

The scope for improving the terms of bank lending to developing countries also appears to be limited, essentially because banks have liabilities that are fixed in money terms and are therefore constrained to seek assets with a similar property. They could, and in our view should, offer reimbursable interest-averaging caps and variable maturity loans (Bergsten, Cline, and Williamson 1985, options 10 and 11). But more fundamental departures from the traditional terms of lending to developing countries seem far more likely to develop in the capital markets, whose participants include a much wider array of institutions and individuals, many of which do not face the accounting constraints on accepting more innovative assets that the banks do.

EXPANDED USE OF THE CAPITAL MARKETS

As noted in section 2, *floating rate notes* (FRNs) have come to constitute an increasing proportion of new issues on the international bond markets, reaching 35 percent in 1984. A number of developing countries already have access to the market: they are almost all in Asia, and are virtually identical to those that could also raise additional loans voluntarily from the commercial banks. The main advantage of selling FRNs rather than borrowing from the banks is that margins are somewhat finer. This can largely be explained by the fact that bonds, unlike bank credits, have not to date been subject to rescheduling (despite the efforts of some banks to include bonds in rescheduling packages). Thus, the additional degree of freedom provided to developing countries by the existence of the FRN market is very limited; it enables those countries that are perceived as creditworthy by the markets to borrow on somewhat cheaper terms, in return for some loss of flexibility should conditions turn adverse. To some extent, the growth of the FRN market is simply the obverse to the cutback in syndicated credits, as individual banks seek to reduce their exposure to rescheduling by shifting into assets that have (at least so far) been exempt from the process.

The market for *long-term fixed-interest bonds* has for many years been closed to developing countries, except indirectly through World Bank borrowing. However, as noted earlier, the impact of this absence is likely to be reduced through the emergence of interest-rate swaps, which will allow creditworthy developing-country borrowers to convert floating-rate obligations into fixed-rate ones. In any event, it is not clear that a return to such fixed-rate borrowing is of great importance. With current interest-rate, currency, and price-level uncertainty, long-term fixed-rate borrowing has relatively poor hedge characteristics for most developing countries. Long-term obligations with smoothed real repayments, such as index-linked bonds, or those with obligations that more closely match elements of developing-country earnings, such as commodity-linked bonds (both of which are discussed below), appear much more promising.

Most of the alternatives to syndicated bank credits discussed up to this point—including NIFs, marketable bank loans, sale of MDB participations (though not cofinancing), FRNs, and debentures—represent moves toward securitization. They would tend to shift the financing of developing countries from the commercial banks, where it has been dominated by a few key players, to securities markets, which are much more atomistic and anonymous. Such a shift has several important implications, some positive and some negative. On the positive side, it reduces the exposure of developing countries to adverse developments in the banking sector, provides them with the potential for more competitive pricing, and increases the range of potential terms, including maturities. On the negative side, it reduces after-the-fact flexibility, since securities markets lack the mechanisms for collective response that the banks have been able to develop in recent years. This flexibility has been extremely important in allowing several major borrowers to get over the hump through rescheduling, and it should not be dismissed lightly.

A number of the possibilities discussed above, notably an expansion in the scope of risk capital and stand-alone finance, would tend to provide greater ex ante matching of debt-service obligations with borrowers' capacity to pay, and thus compensate for a reduction in after-the-fact flexibility resulting from the securitization of general obligation credits. Similarly, if and when options markets develop to the point of providing an alternative route for developing countries to reduce their exposure to unexpected variations in receipts and payments, it will be possible to view any loss of flexibility from securitization with greater equanimity. To the extent that neither of those developments occur, however, it would be crucial to incorporate more before-the-fact flexibility in securities sold on the markets, to compensate for any reduction in the role of the banks.

One possible way of accomplishing this would be through the sale of *index-linked bonds*. Such bonds provide that the value of the principal be regularly revised upward in line with a specified price index. Interest payments are also increased in line with inflation: this is accomplished automatically if capital values are revised just before interest payments fall due.

A number of countries, including Brazil and Britain, have issued index-linked bonds in their domestic markets in recent years. Although indexation has been justly charged with a pernicious role in accelerating and perpetuating inflation in Brazil (see, for example, Williamson 1985), it is indexation of *factor incomes* rather than *long-term savings instruments* that created the problem. In Britain there is general agreement that, by broadening the range of assets available, issues of index-linked bonds have enabled the government to reduce its borrowing costs.

There appear to be no instances to date of indexed international bonds, although an attempt has been made to interest at least one sovereign borrower in issuing Bulldog bonds linked to the British retail price index. The reasons for this absence are far from self-evident. One can understand the reluctance of financial institutions that issue liquid claims with fixed nominal values (like banks) to place a part of their assets in index-linked bonds that can vary in nominal terms in the short run. But there are also many investors—private, corporate, endowment, and some long-term institutional investors—whose primary concern must be with the real value of their portfolios, and earnings, in the long run. Similarly, most long-term borrowers should be concerned primarily with the real long-term value of their debt-service obligations, and these will tend to be less uncertain with an indexed asset than with a conventional floating rate note, let alone a conventional fixed-interest bond. Naturally the attractions of indexed assets are less as inflation subsides than they were in the 1970s, but even now the level of inflation is far from negligible—and its future course remains uncertain.

This is not to claim that developing countries are likely to be able to issue "ideal" index-linked bonds, with a link to their own export prices. It is more likely that they might be able to issue bonds linked to the prices of certain specified commodities that they export: that is, to issue commodity-linked bonds (see below). But a general index to their own export prices would be difficult to define unambiguously, and would in any event not have any appealing properties to investors. It would therefore be necessary to employ a price index of the country in which the bond was issued. By issuing indexed bonds in several currencies, a borrower could obtain a liability structure that helped offset its trade and other financial exposure. Alternatively, Eurobonds might be issued in a composite currency unit, like the ECU or SDR, with indexation using a weighted average of the inflation rates of the countries whose currencies compose the basket.

While indexed bonds would provide borrowers with the best protection against variations in inflation and the real interest rate, they are disliked by many institutional investors to whom a degree of stability in nominal receipts is important. An adaptation of the floating rate note, called the *constant-real-payment floating rate note* (its mortgage cousin is called the constant-payment-factor variable rate mortgage: see Modigliani and Lessard 1975), comes close to reconciling the desire of borrowers to smooth the path of real debt-service obligations with the desire of lenders to receive a relatively constant stream of nominal income. It achieves this by making use of two separate rates: a debiting factor, which is the interest charge on the outstanding balance, and a payment factor, which is the amount that the borrower has to pay each period.

The debiting factor would be set in each period with reference to a standard market interest rate like LIBOR, just as in a standard FRN. Intermediaries with liabilities carrying a floating interest rate would therefore find such assets acceptable. The payment factor would be chosen with a view to yielding equal real repayments over the life of the contract. This could of course be done exactly only if future real interest rates were known, but moderate errors in the assumptions regarding the future real interest rate would not lead to major deviations from constant real payments. Moreover, errors caused by mistaken forecasts of real interest rates will cancel out over time; for example, too high a forecast would accelerate repayments, which would reduce the outstanding principal and thus reduce future repayments.

This formula could lead to a payment factor less than the debiting factor in the early years of the loan, under conditions of high inflation. That is, amortization would be negative and the principal outstanding would increase. This would simply serve to correct one of the distortions that high inflation produces in repayment streams under standard loan instruments.

Recently instruments of this type have been launched on a small scale in mortgage financing, but they have not been applied to corporate or country borrowing.[33]

A *commodity-linked bond* would specify that interest or amortization payments or both would vary with the price of a commodity, or a specified basket of commodities. The commodity (or commodities) involved would need to have well-defined prices that are unambiguously determined in a competitive market, but provided that this condition was satisfied—as it is for several dozen commodities that collectively comprise a major part of developing-country exports—there would be no technical difficulty in drawing up such a contract (Lessard 1977, 1983).

There have been some precedents for bonds of this sort, not all of them particularly happy. Perhaps the most famous are French gold-linked bonds, most recently issued by Giscard d'Estaing when Minister of Finance in the early 1970s. These proved astronomically expensive to service after the great rise in the gold price during the 1970s. Since France neither mined gold nor planned to dispose of its stocks, the issue of such bonds was essentially speculation by the French Treasury, rather than the hedging operation that would be entailed by a developing country issuing bonds with a return linked to the prices of the commodities that it sells. A more relevant experience, since it did involve hedging, is that of Sunshine Mining, which mines silver and in 1980 issued bonds with a yield linked to the price of silver. The IFC has also participated in financings with commodity-linked equity "kickers" on a private placement basis for borrowers in Mexico and Peru.

The other major precedent is the Mexican oil-linked bonds issued in 1977.

---

33. However, a very similar approach has been used to compute the repayments due by the Mexican private sector for the foreign loans taken over by the Banco de Mexico. The formula used aims to produce a stream of repayments each of which has the same present value. The payment factor (A) is computed by the formula

$$A = \frac{P}{n} \prod_{t=1}^{n} (1 + i_t)$$

where P is the principal outstanding, n is the number of periods to maturity, and i_t is the interest rate or debiting factor that will, or is expected to, prevail in period t. If future interest rates are known with certainty, the payment factor rises at the rate of interest. If the debiting factor is a floating interest rate, deviations of actual from expected rates produce some distortions in the ideal time stream of payments. This formula also allows for negative amortization in the early years of a loan since the payment may be below the calculated interest charge.

These had a peso yield coupled with a redemption value linked to the dollar price of oil, but translated into pesos at the official exchange rate and paid in pesos. Such bonds not unnaturally fell into disfavor with foreign investors when Mexico responded to its financial difficulties in 1982 by calculating the peso value of the proceeds at the overvalued official exchange rate, but only allowing conversion of pesos to dollars at the far less favorable black market rate. But that hardly provides a precedent that justifies dismissing the feasibility of commodity-linked bonds issued on the international market and with debt-service payments due in dollars.

The objective of issuing commodity-linked bonds would be to enable the borrowing country to hedge its risks. A major factor contributing to the debt crisis was the coincidence of the rise in debt-service obligations and the decline in the earnings of commodity exports with which to service debts. With commodity-linked bonds, debt-service obligations would have fallen in parallel with commodity prices, thus providing relief from cash-flow difficulties.

It is sometimes suggested that countries could buy themselves such insurance in a different way by entering the futures markets. That may become possible one day, but at the moment those markets are too short term to provide an effective alternative. Similarly, options may in the future provide an alternative, but they do not at the moment.

Of course, commodity-linked bonds reduce the risk of debt-servicing difficulties to the issuer only if the commodity to which payments are linked is one that the issuer will be selling in world markets—as was not true of the French gold-linked bonds. But most developing countries produce some primary products which they export on a significant scale without having excessive market power (which might introduce an element of moral hazard, although it is difficult to believe this would be large—it is most unlikely that a country would benefit by reducing its export receipts so as to cut its debt-service payments).

One would expect that in general commodity-linked bonds would need to carry a higher *expected* yield when issued than conventional bonds, since the purchaser would be accepting a payments stream with more uncertainty. The borrower would be compensated for this in two ways. First, his debt-service obligations would vary with his ability to pay, thus reducing the danger of a future credit crunch. Second, this link between obligations and ability to pay should reassure lenders regarding the capacity of a debtor to service a given volume of debt, and thus persuade them to lend more than they would be willing to do on conventional terms. An extreme case would arise if the market judged that a country could not be safely entrusted with any new debt on conventional terms, but was prepared to lend with the knowledge that repayment obligations would be concentrated on periods when the country was in a particularly favorable position to honor them.

Commodity-linked general obligations might be issued as part of a general debt refinancing exercise. A country such as Nigeria or Peru with significant dependence on a key export might replace a portion of its general obligations with commodity-linked instruments entailing lower current debt service, in return for a step-up in debt service should such prices increase beyond a prespecified level. Since such instruments provide holders with an option to gain from higher prices, it is likely that they would reduce current debt service even in the case of a commodity such as oil where the price is not expected to increase in the short term. The reason for this is that prices are sufficiently volatile that there is a substantial chance that the holder will gain from an increase in prices and, if not, the initial yield will provide a floor.[34]

Two sorts of investors might be expected to show an interest in acquiring commodity-linked bonds. One group would be those who wished to back a hunch regarding future commodity price trends. The other group would be those who wished to hedge against increased costs of their own inputs.

It has been suggested, notably by Norman Bailey (1983), that debtor countries should seek to replace their bank loans by "exchange participation notes." These would entitle their holders to a specified share in the issuing country's export earnings. A major objection to this proposal is that it would supply the banks with assets that are not well-suited to them, since they might initially sell at a deep discount and would subsequently offer a fluctuating return quite unrelated to that on the banks' liabilities (Bergsten, Cline, and Williamson 1985, option 18). However, the same objection would not apply to bonds placed on the international capital market with a return linked to the value of the country's exports. Such bonds may be termed *trade-linked bonds*.

This proposal offers both advantages and disadvantages as compared to

---

34. The Mexican petrobonds had this option element and were priced with an initial yield of 10 percent in pesos at a time when straight bonds with comparable currency and country-risk exposures, such as those issued by Teléfonos de Mexico, were yielding some 15 percent. For an excellent introduction to the pricing of option elements in financial instruments see Merton and Mason (1984).

the proposal for commodity-linked bonds. The principal advantage is that it would yield a closer correspondence between a country's obligations and its ability to pay. A second advantage is that the creditors would acquire an interest in the developed countries permitting market access for the exports of the borrower. But there are two important disadvantages as well. The first relates to the problem of moral hazard: if a country built up a significant volume of external debt in this form, the desire to restrain debt-service payments might become a significant argument against a vigorous policy of export promotion. The second concerns the potential market for such bonds: it is much easier to believe that there might be a significant body of investors willing to speculate or hedge on the future price of copper than to speculate on the future export revenues of Chile or Zambia. Because of these complexities, such instruments might require some form of pooling and guarantee, such as the one outlined below for index-linked bonds.

This proposal for ex ante linkage to exports (or, in the case of commodity bonds, to prices of specific commodities) should not be confused with the ex post linkage of debt service to exports announced by Peru. The latter involves a partial repudiation of previously contracted debt, the problems of which are analyzed in Bergsten, Cline, and Williamson (1985, option 17), while the former involves the design of a voluntary contract acceptable to both lender and borrower. Of course, there is little question but that Peru would now be better off had it contracted for such contingent repayments at some point in the past.

Of these proposals for modifying general obligation financing to secure a closer matching of debt-service requirements with borrowers' ability to pay, we judge that index-linked bonds and commodity-linked bonds offer the greatest potential improvement for borrowers. However, we also have to note that both ideas have been on the table for some time with little result. (Indeed, each of the authors of this study began championing one of them in 1977!) We believe there are two reasons for their failure to date.

First, few developing countries have taken a sufficiently long view of the implications of their liability structure to wish to incorporate such innovations. Most have acted opportunistically, borrowing on whatever terms were most readily available. Many, including Peru, now have powerful reasons to regret their past negligence.

Second, financial markets are reluctant to accept innovations unless these are initially introduced by names with the highest standing in credit markets. Since both instruments represent a substantial departure from existing patterns of finance, coupled with relatively long maturities, it is unlikely that they could be introduced by any single developing country without significant initial costs and, notably, the backing of one or more OECD governments or MDBs.

This suggests that, in order to exploit these innovations, developing countries are going to need help, both in financial analysis and planning and in the issuing of the securities. Several different mechanisms are possible, ranging from guaranteed single-country issues to borrowing and subsequent onlending by an MDB on an index- or commodity-linked basis.

For example, Williamson's original proposal for the issue of index-linked bonds envisaged that an international financial institution (one of the MDBs, or conceivably the IMF) would act as the agent for a consortium of developing countries in floating long-term, indexed, partially guaranteed bonds on the world capital market.[35] Each issue of bonds would be the joint liability of the particular group of countries that expressed a desire to borrow at the time of issue, in proportions determined by their willingness to service debt at the real interest rate set at the time of issue. This interest rate, along with the quantity sold and the distribution of both borrowers and lenders, would be determined each quarter (for example) by a sealed-bid auction that served to equate supply and demand.

Such bonds might be denominated either in a leading international currency like the dollar or in a composite currency unit like the SDR. Dollar-denominated bonds would be indexed to a measure of US inflation, such as the US wholesale price index or the GDP deflator. SDR-denominated bonds would be indexed with a weighted average of similar measures (for example, nonfood WPIs) of the inflation rates in the five countries whose currencies compose the SDR basket, the weights being the same as those of the currencies in the basket.

The scheme was proposed as a way of enabling sovereign borrowers to attract long-term external finance, in the form of general balance of payments loans, from OPEC surplus countries or nonbank private-sector lenders, on terms—notably a fixed real interest rate—that match the needs of long-term

---

35. In at least two recent compilations of proposals to relieve the debt crisis this proposal has been described as the "UK Treasury Scheme," doubtless to the dismay of H.M. Treasury; it derived its name from the fact that the author in question persuaded the House of Commons Select Committee on the Treasury and Civil Service to give the proposal an airing and faint blessing in its 1983 "Report on International Lending by Banks."

borrowers. A major difficulty would doubtless be posed by the need to provide a credible guarantee. It was envisaged that the partial guarantee would be organized by establishing a guarantee fund that would assure creditors that they would receive the full interest and amortization due them for as long as the guarantee fund was solvent, even if the debtors failed to service their debts on time. If there were major debt defaults, the guarantee fund would be exhausted and the lenders would lose, but the scheme was based on the premise that markets would treat such a disaster scenario as such a remote contingency that a limited guarantee fund would suffice to ensure that the bonds were classified as low-risk assets. Criticisms voiced in subsequent discussion have concerned not so much the realism of this assumption, but rather where the money to finance the guarantee fund would come from.

It would be appropriate to expect borrowers to pay a modest insurance premium into the guarantee fund, perhaps geared in some way to their performance. But a fairly substantial nucleus would also be required immediately. Since the IMF's gold stock is now redundant, it might be worth contemplating the possibility of using it for this purpose. A more straightforward approach would be to appeal to the governments of the donor countries to provide guarantees that would permit the launching of the scheme. The leverage provided by such guarantees should be high, although it would be impossible to know how high until the scheme had been operating for some time.

The main reason for proposing that these bonds be launched on a collective basis involving the joint obligations of a group of developing countries, rather than that individual countries should sell indexed bonds, concerns the need for guarantee arrangements. It is difficult to imagine donors offering guarantees to individual countries, let alone borrowers paying premia to a national guarantee fund. Moreover, since a country that defaults is more likely to default 100 percent rather than partially, a partial national guarantee fund would not greatly reduce the probability of suffering loss through default, but merely limit the extent of loss should the default occur. In contrast, a partial guarantee fund supporting the liabilities of a group of countries would suffice to eliminate any risk of loss except in the extreme, and presumably extremely improbable, contingency of a series of defaults. That is, the insurance principle could be brought to bear for a collective scheme, but not for a national scheme.

5   Policy Initiatives

We concluded in section 2 that the present outlook is for inadequate flows of nonconcessional finance to developing countries for the remainder of the decade, and that there would be substantial advantages in extra lending of $15 billion to $20 billion a year. We argued in section 3 that the present structure of the stock of outstanding debt leaves much to be desired. In the previous section we reviewed a number of instruments, actual and potential, that might be capable of augmenting the flow and improving the structure. The remaining task is that of identifying policy initiatives that might diminish the gap between the desirable and the probable.

It would be unrealistic to expect to be able to attract vast quantities of capital quickly into instruments that are not already in widespread use. Markets will take time to accept innovations, and they will insist on seeing an established track record before being willing to commit more than token sums. It is nonetheless important to start building that track record immediately, so as to create the chance of achieving a major change in structure in the 1990s.

Of the instruments discussed above that are not already in widespread use, we would think it ought to be possible to induce meaningful flows of, say, $1 billion to $2 billion a year each in equity investment, quasi-equities, stand-alone loans, indexed bonds, and conceivably commodity-linked bonds. This would give a total flow of $4 billion to $10 billion a year, of which one would expect that the bulk would come from institutional investors (pension funds and insurance companies) and a substantial chunk (especially in quasi-equities) from the corporate sector. These estimates are shown in table 9. The structure of lending that would result from the more optimistic end of the range is shown by the column labeled "Alternative 1987" in figure 1.

It is conceivable that even larger sums might be achievable if some of these instruments catch on, but it would be unwise to rely on that. Hence it is also necessary to seek to expand the resources flowing from existing lenders. Of these, the source that has often been looked to as something of a panacea is direct investment. Our view is that further liberalization by the host countries might marginally stimulate the flow, by perhaps $1 billion to $2 billion a year, but that it would be unrealistic to expect much more than that. Liberalization by the host countries might also attract more investment

T A B L E 9   **Potential sources of expanded capital flows to developing**
countries, late 1980s (billion dollars)

	Amount
Innovative private sources	4–10
Equity investment	1–2
Quasi-equities	1–2
Stand-alone finance	1–2
Indexed bonds	1–2
Commodity-linked bonds	0–2
Traditional private sources	2–4
Direct investment	1–2
Real estate	1–2
Public sector	6–9
SDR allocations	3
Accelerated disbursements	2
Expansion of World Bank lending	1–4
Target	15–20

Source: Estimates in text.

in real estate, perhaps of a similar order of magnitude. As far as the commercial banks are concerned, the struggle will be to achieve the $15 billion embodied in the base projection.

The most optimistic count would thus be that the private sector might come close to achieving our minimum target for increased capital flows. To do that would require active support from the international financial institutions in such spheres as cofinancing quasi-equities and launching indexed bonds. A more skeptical assessment might doubt whether these sources would raise more than some $6 billion a year, only 40 percent of our minimum target. Moreover, even if the sums raised by the new instruments proved to be toward the top end of the range, this might not all represent a net addition to the flow: for example, commercial banks might lend on a stand-alone basis, but cut back even further on syndicated credits.

The existence of this large potential gap points to a need for expanded use of the international financial institutions, especially over the next few years while they are nurturing the growth of the private sector that may ultimately come to play the major role. On a longer-term basis, we envisage their playing a key role in helping to unbundle risks. We return to our proposals for expanding their role at the end of this section.

One point of view holds that if something is not already being done by the markets it must be because it is not worth doing. Obviously we do not accept that contention or we would not have embarked on the present study. But at the same time we certainly accept that if something is not being done already it is probably because one of the relevant parties—the governments of the developing or industrial countries, private financial institutions, and multilateral institutions—is not persuaded that it is desirable. (Just occasionally there may be a case where something is not being done because no one has thought of it.) So we turn now to identifying where the interests of the parties involved lie and to pointing to where in our judgment a realistic appraisal of interests would suggest the need for action.

Developing-Country Governments

We deal first with the governments of developing countries to reflect a conviction that the major responsibility for improving the investment climate must lie with the borrowers themselves. In the course of the study we have had cause to note the ambiguous attitudes of many of the borrowers' governments with regard to direct investment and their negative attitude to foreign equity investment—to which one could add a lack of enthusiasm for MIGA, a dismissal of the proposal to issue indexed bonds at a time when it could have provided some insurance against a debt crisis, and a marked reluctance to enter cofinancing arrangements with the World Bank except when creditworthiness is in question.

In section 3 we suggested that these attitudes had probably been nurtured by a systematic underestimation of risks, especially those associated with the production of primary commodities. The great postwar boom avoided commodity price declines comparable to those of the 1930s, perhaps in part because a general commitment to Keynesian economic management prevented prolonged recessions. Moreover, when developing countries did encounter economic difficulties, the international community made an effort to limit their impact. All this changed in the 1980s. The key question that the developing countries need to ask themselves is whether it was the 1980s, or the earlier postwar period, that was the historical aberration. Unless one confidently answers that it was the former, one is bound to conclude that prudence dictates an attempt to reduce risk exposure, either by restructuring debt or by exploiting markets such as those for options, even though the expected cost is bound to be higher. That is certainly our view.

In short, the developing countries need to make a more realistic appraisal of the risks inherent in their own economies, as well as those to which they are exposed by virtue of their international financial commitments. They should carefully assess their comparative advantage in bearing such risks and develop financial strategies at the national, enterprise, and project level that shift risks and hedge exposures in line with their assessment. In evaluating programs or projects, depending on whether their assessment of comparative advantage calls for retaining the risks entailed or laying them off, they should adjust expected benefits for the contribution of such undertakings to the variability of national income or the risk premium demanded by world financial markets for laying off such risks.

Most discussions have assumed that the only significant sources of private finance are loans from the commercial banks and direct investment, and have therefore urged that the decline in the former be offset by a greater effort by the host countries to attract the latter. This is in general good advice: although there are instances where a country might legitimately seek to restrict direct investment (for example, where a multinational is large enough to dominate a small market so that its expansion, especially via takeover, would curtail competition), some of the limitations on inward investment seem to have been driven by xenophobia or paranoia rather than by economic calculation. Attitudes on this score are to some extent changing already. Moreover, the export-led growth model that is newly popular in Latin America may persuade some multinationals to consider more extensive use of their subsidiaries in that region to export to other areas. And as economic growth recovers in the developing countries, the traditional incentive to multinationals to expand so as to exploit their company-specific expertise in a growing home market will once again come into play. The process may usefully be reinforced by existing investment-guarantee agencies as well as MIGA, if this is indeed approved at last.

Useful as direct investment may be, however, it would be paradoxical if it again assumed a dominant role in capital flows, at least in the more advanced developing countries. After all, direct investment is generally motivated by the desire to exploit some form of intangible capital in a foreign market. Some forms of intangible capital that may provide a basis for profitable inward investment at the initial stages of development—notably entrepreneurship—cease to yield rents to foreign investors as development proceeds. The role of direct investment will probably be increasingly concentrated in industries requiring sophisticated technology and know-how or exploiting well-known trademarks. Hence we allow only $1 billion to $2 billion a year for the increase in direct investment that would be likely to result from a more welcoming posture by the host countries.

As development proceeds, at least in a basically capitalist framework, it becomes increasingly natural to expect that a part of the capital inflow will take the form of equity investment. Such investment requires significant local preconditions: large, privately owned firms, a viable securities law, and a functioning stock exchange. While much scope remains for improvement in these respects in many countries, the biggest obstacle to increased equity investment is often that it is excluded by existing regulations, sometimes unintentionally but often deliberately. All countries with an active stock exchange (table 6) that restrict foreign purchase, holding, or sale of equities, whether by outright prohibition, by minimum holding periods, by excessive withholding taxes, or by restricting the right to repatriate the proceeds of sales through the same exchange market used to switch funds in, would be well advised to consider whether their restrictions should not be liberalized.

As pointed out in section 4, this could be done without posing any threat of surrendering national control to foreigners, either by introducing a separate class of B-shares to which foreign holdings are limited, or by legislating maximum percentages of permitted foreign holdings. If countries are worried about potential outflows of money that has been invested in stocks, they should at least encourage the establishment of foreign investment funds which avoid this danger, on the model already adopted by Brazil, Korea, Mexico, Taiwan, and Thailand. The International Finance Corporation is able and willing to help set up such funds.

The midst of an economic crisis, with a much undervalued currency and a collapse in stock prices, would not have been an opportune time to liberalize foreign access to domestic equities (or, for that matter, real estate); it would have smacked of a "fire sale." Fortunately the main debtor countries have experienced booming stock markets in the last two years and are now safely past that stage.

One particularly anomalous discouragement to equity investment concerns pension funds established for the benefit of local employees by multinational companies. Some countries treat such funds as foreign investors and forbid their purchase of local equities.

It is of course difficult to form any precise estimate of the size of the funds that might be tapped by a more positive attitude to foreign equity investment. On the one hand, the present stake of foreign investors is minuscule (estimated at $750 million). On the other hand, the total stock of equity assets is substantial (now probably over $100 billion even excluding the marginal countries like Singapore). Furthermore, international intra-OECD equity investment is increasing dramatically, and similar forces are leading investment managers to examine non-OECD markets carefully, if still with some skepticism. The annual increase in foreign portfolio investment will probably be well over $10 billion by the late 1980s. It would not seem impossible for the developing countries to capture 10 percent of that increase if they set out to try to: hence our figure of $1 billion to $2 billion a year as a plausible range for what might be achieved.

In addition to direct and equity investment, there is a strong case for the governments of developing countries to welcome a number of the other instruments discussed in section 4. As already noted, however, it seems unlikely that these countries could independently pioneer the introduction of novel instruments like index-linked or commodity-linked bonds. Historically, financial markets have accepted financial innovations only when these have initially been introduced by names with the highest standing in the credit markets. This suggests that the developing countries are going to need help, from the governments of some of the industrial countries or the international organizations or both, in establishing markets for new instruments like these that offer a better international distribution of risk. Suggestions to that end are advanced below.

If and when markets for such assets do develop, the developing countries should be quick to exploit them. The OPEC countries would be a natural constituency for some of these instruments, notably quasi-equities like revenue sharing, since their features are consistent with the tenets of Islamic banking. Indeed, it may well be that some of the Islamic financial institutions would be able to contribute valuable know-how to the design of these instruments.

Similarly, the developing countries are unlikely to be able to impose on the banks a switch to forms of bank lending that offer a more appropriate time stream of debt-service payments (variable maturity loans, RIACs, or constant-real-interest floating rate notes, which could smooth real debt-service payments almost as effectively as index-linked bonds). Once again, however, they should exploit markets for such assets if and when these develop and they should grasp any willingness that the banks may display to offer more appropriate loan terms for a reasonable addition to the spread. The swap and options markets may also come to offer opportunities for improving the currency denomination of debt-service streams so as to improve their hedge characteristics.

A major cause of the difficulties of a number of debtor countries has been the export of capital by their own citizens. Enders and Mattione (1984, table 5) estimate that capital flight summed to $14.3 billion in Argentina, $15.2 billion in Mexico, and $13.0 billion in Venezuela, a total of $42.5 billion, from 1979 through 1982. The sums were much more modest in other debtor countries, but nonetheless probably significant enough to have materially aggravated their problems. The *Federal Reserve Bulletin* (August 1985, table 3.17) estimates that US bank liabilities to Latin America totaled $55 billion in April 1985. These figures suggest that the net debt of Latin America to US banks is much smaller than implied by the figures usually quoted. In part this is no accident: it is apparently common practice for a Latin businessman who has built up a precautionary balance in Miami to use this as collateral for a back-to-back loan, which he then has the right to service through the foreign-exchange market—without losing the security of a deposit in a US bank account.

For several Latin countries, the debt crisis would be over if they could secure a major reversal of past capital flight. But this is easier recognized than achieved. Realistic macroeconomic policies, involving competitive real exchange rates and positive real interest rates, along with the avoidance of penal taxation, are undoubtedly essential preconditions for stopping, and ipso facto for reversing, capital flight. Exchange control can help to limit it but not to reverse it; indeed, if anything, exchange control will discourage the repatriation of capital, by creating fears of the difficulty of getting out again if things go wrong.

Apart from the stimulus of misconceived macroeconomic policies, the other major spur to capital flight is the attraction of being able to earn interest free of tax. Interest earned by nonresidents on US bank accounts has long been free of US tax, and in 1984 a similar exemption was granted the holders of bonds by elimination of withholding tax. Where home governments levy tax according to the residence principle (which is not true of all Latin governments), tax on foreign interest income is in principle due in their home country, but it is at the moment voluntary, and therefore unpaid, since the home country has no way of learning about the income unless the recipient chooses to declare it. The United States is willing to provide information on interest earnings to countries with which it has concluded double-taxation treaties, but these exclude the Latin American countries, with which it has major differences in tax philosophy. In particular, the Latins have been unwilling to reduce withholding taxes on the dividends and fees of US multinationals and the United States has been unwilling to recognize Latin tax incentives (through "tax sparing").

In the past the pecuniary self-interest of the Latins coincided with their tax philosophy, so it was easy for them to resist US approaches to conclude double-taxation treaties. The balance of advantage is less clear now, with the large volume of Latin funds held in the United States. Nevertheless, although most flight capital from Latin America has gone to the United States, it is not clear that a tax treaty with the United States alone would suffice. It would not be difficult to shift funds from the United States to Europe or the Caribbean if their owners perceived advantages in doing so. The chances of being able to conclude tax treaties on a sufficiently comprehensive basis to make a real impact seem remote. The whole area of international fiscal cooperation is one that seems overdue for a comprehensive study with a view to seeking a rational international tax regime backed up by an international agreement, but the area is so complex that it would be quite unrealistic to look for any relief to the problems caused by capital flight from that source in the near term.

Developing countries will increasingly need to compete internationally for domestic savings as well as for foreign capital. Investors seek the highest possible return consistent with a given degree of risk, and, just like investors in industrial countries, those in developing countries are becoming ever more aware of opportunities on a worldwide basis as financial markets become increasingly linked. Nevertheless, it is reasonable to expect that citizens would be more willing to repatriate their funds than foreigners would be to invest on a comparable scale, provided that conditions were perceived to be broadly competitive with those on world markets.

Where assets held abroad have not been acquired illegally, it might be worth following the Indian example and creating a mutual fund accessible only to nationals. Deposits in the fund could be granted immunity against any future decision to impose exchange control—a promise that could be given credibility by placing the management of the fund under the control of a foreign agent, such as an investment bank, and granting the fund the status of a foreign investor.

A difficult problem could be posed by the need to find the right balance between assuring investors the right to withdraw their funds in foreign exchange in case of need and assuring the country that its flight capital has returned for good. Recycling flight capital to a debtor country would not be of much use to it if the capital were free to fly away again at the first whiff of trouble. In normal times this would not be a problem: the desire of some investors to liquidate assets would be matched by new deposits and earnings from the assets held by the fund, with a cushion of liquid assets held outside the sponsoring country adequate to finance temporary imbalances. But, at times of political uncertainty or payments difficulties, there might well be a net desire to withdraw foreign exchange from the fund.

To meet this problem one might distinguish between low-yielding deposits, which would carry the right to withdraw at par, and high-yielding shares, whose price would be variable. The redemption price of the shares at any time might be determined in at least two ways. One would be to treat the shares in the fund as a closed-end mutual fund, so that a net desire to sell shares would cause a fall in their price of whatever magnitude was needed to eliminate the excess supply. The other would be to provide that withdrawals would be possible at par only in local currency, with translation into foreign exchange being undertaken at the parallel rate.

An alternative scheme, adopted recently by Chile, allows local investors holding funds offshore to purchase that country's external obligations (typically at a discount) and exchange them at face value for local currency to be used to purchase the equity of local firms. While such an arrangement poses many monitoring difficulties, it is attractive in that it simultaneously achieves an exchange of debt for equity and the repatriation of flight capital. Thus, the country gains a sounder financial structure without ceding further control to foreign interests. Argentina has also recently declared an amnesty for those who repatriate their capital.

Whether countries where capital export was illegal would feel happy following such an approach is more problematical. But Colombia, for example, has adopted a scheme that permits residents to import without receiving an allocation of foreign exchange, in return for a modest surcharge, in order to tap its residents' holdings of foreign capital.

Industrial Country Governments

The debt crisis was a joint consequence of the vulnerable situation in which the developing countries placed themselves through excessive general obligation borrowing and the abrupt switch in policy toward combating inflation that the industrial countries made in 1979–82. However necessary the switch may have been, it is a fact that a disproportionate part of the costs were borne by the developing countries. The industrial countries have so far done remarkably little to relieve those costs. It is time that they did more than provide the minimal emergency packages needed to prevent the system from collapsing.

Action is called for in at least four areas: to enable the multilateral institutions to play an enhanced role in intermediation, to expand the flow of export credit, to liberalize such rules as impede their private sectors' lending to or investing in the developing countries, and to promote the emergence of markets for new instruments that could improve the structure of developing-country borrowing. These actions are of course additional to the overriding imperative of sustaining macroeconomic and trade policies that will accommodate the balance of payments adjustment policies of the debtor countries.

Multilateral institutions—the IMF, the World Bank group, and the regional development banks—have played an important role in linking the developing countries with world financial markets. Their role should be enhanced in order to support a number of the innovations outlined in section 4. But this need not be accomplished by big injections of public money. Given the present political mood in the major industrial countries, calls to that effect are unlikely to be heeded anyway. Furthermore, such additional funds as the taxpayers may be willing to put up for supporting development through the multilateral institutions should be channeled to organizations with a proven record of effective action to help the poorest, such as the International Fund for Agricultural Development and the International Development Association. We therefore start from the premise that support for intermediation to developing countries in general through the multilateral institutions should not require a significant increase in current transfers.

Such a constraint leaves much scope for constructive action, if these institutions seek to apply their resources where they have the greatest comparative advantage and provided at least that it is not interpreted as ruling out an increase in the World Bank's callable (but not paid-in) capital, a proposal that won almost unanimous support at the last Bank-Fund Annual Meetings (although near-unanimity seems not to be enough when the odd man out is the United States). Indeed, much could be done even without increasing the Bank's capital. For example, guarantees can be provided to cover noncommercial risks in which the Bank has special competence due to its preferred-creditor status and its policy influence through regular consultations, thus permitting projects to be financed on a quasi-equity or stand-alone basis. In view of the limited risks involved such guarantees could legitimately count less than one-for-one against the Bank's capital. In addition, the Bank can innovate in its own loan terms, offering a choice of currency composition and interest caps, for a market price determined by its costs in entering the relevant swap and options markets.

Nevertheless, we believe that a substantial capital increase is also justified. Such an increase is needed to allow the Bank to expand its project, sector, and structural adjustment lending, especially over the next few years while the debt crisis is being overcome, and until the innovative forms of financing recommended in this study have had a chance to build up. We endeavor below to develop a rough estimate of the scale of the increase that would be called for to enable the Bank to play these key roles. Although the IFC has just had its capital doubled, we attach such importance to its operations that we would also support an early initiative for a further major increase.

Furthermore, in one particular context we believe that a modest additional injection of public funds should be sanctioned. We argued in section 4 that the most promising proposals for improved bond finance, involving index-linked and commodity-linked bonds, were unlikely to get off the ground without active support by the industrial countries. In the case of collective issues of index-linked bonds, the critical support would take the form of endowment of a guarantee fund, sufficient at least to support a pilot program capable of establishing how large the leverage provided by such funds might prove to be.

In addition to increasing the scale of their operations, the MDBs should also increase the scope of their activities in various qualitative dimensions. The critical point for the industrial countries to recognize is that their own internal private financial markets depend to a great extent on the institutional infrastructure, and that institutional support is of even greater importance in the international setting given the inherent limitations of international contracts. Thus, the activities of the MDBs should not be seen as supplanting private capital flows, but as complementary and helping to create circumstances under which these flows can be of greatest mutual benefit.

A second area calling for more supportive policies by a number of industrial countries concerns the provision and guarantee of export credit. Until the 1960s this was one of the three major sources of external capital for developing countries (figure 1), and it still constitutes around 20 percent of the outstanding stock of developing-country debt. Some writers have even looked to the export credit agencies as the natural source from which to seek additional credit flows to compensate for the cutback in bank lending, on the ground that the export lobbies in the industrial countries constitute the most promising source of political support for expanding capital flows to developing countries (Bolin and Del Canto 1983, Lever 1983). Certainly, many borrowers would welcome a chance to substitute export credits for the bank loans that are no longer available. But in fact many export credit agencies have cut back since the onset of the debt crisis: insured export credits have been subject to a record number of Paris Club reschedulings, and these reschedulings and their attendant financial claims have weakened the financial position of the agencies.

Many export credit agencies have extended their coverage to the export of services. Clearly, given the importance of transactions in services, especially the transfer of technology and management skills, this trend should be encouraged. It might be extended further to cover incentive contracts where payment is linked to some measure of commercial success. The extension of export guarantees to services should be complemented by making investment guarantees against noncommercial risks available to quasi-equity investments and project financing.

Two general criticisms can be made of the past operation of these agencies. One, perhaps inherent in the nature of such agencies, is that they compromise their standards with regard to project selection and creditworthiness to promote exports. The second is that export credit agencies suffer with a vengeance from the herd instincts of the bankers: they remain willing to provide coverage for debtor countries pursuing rash policies for too long, so as not to jeopardize export business by withdrawing before their competitors, but are reluctant to resume the provision of coverage after adjustment has been set in train.

The first weakness could perhaps be best tackled by expanding the role of the World Bank in cofinancing with export credit agencies, as well as by seeking whenever possible to incorporate incentives to suppliers to ensure that projects are soundly designed and executed. The second would seem to call for a joint resolve, which the OECD might appropriately be charged with seeking, that at a minimum any country having in place an adjustment program approved by the IMF should be eligible for coverage by the export credit agencies of the industrial countries.

The developed countries should also eliminate restrictions that hamper private lending to or investment in developing countries, except where there is a genuine prudential need. Examples include: prohibitions on pension funds from buying the securities of these countries; limits on the proportion of their portfolio that insurance companies can place in such assets; and restrictions on the flotation of developing-country bonds.

In the United States, mutual funds do not face restraints of this type. Private pension funds are governed by the requirements of the Employee Retirement and Income Security Act (ERISA) of 1974. These require that pension funds follow a "prudent man" investment strategy, and managers who do not exhibit due prudence can be sued. For some years this did inhibit foreign investment, and especially investment in developing countries. One way of avoiding the danger of being sued for imprudence is to follow the crowd and invest in the same types of assets as all other investors. If this were the *only* way of satisfying the requirement, presently marginal borrowers such as the developing countries would indeed have cause for complaint. But there is a second way, and that is to do adequate research on the characteristics of the securities bought. It is well accepted that a portfolio can prudently contain securities that are individually risky, provided that they are diversified to a point where the portfolio risk is small. It would not be reasonable to seek any modification of that requirement. Neither is it necessary, given that pension funds have already made the breakthrough into extensive foreign investment (though not yet into extensive investment in developing countries).

In contrast, most state and local pension funds are prohibited by law from investing in foreign securities. In recent years a few states have started to legalize foreign investment, but there is still a long way to go. What is needed here is, of course, action by state legislatures rather than by Congress.

The situation seems to be broadly similar in most other countries in which pension funds are important asset holders. That is, the private sector is relatively free to invest abroad, but public schemes are more constrained. In Japan, foreign investment was prohibited until 1979, when private pension funds were permitted to invest up to 10 percent of their assets abroad. They have vigorously exploited this freedom, and now have over 8 percent of their funds in foreign assets, predominantly in the United States, but with a certain amount in East Asia. There is no legal obstacle to their investing in other developing countries. However, the Japanese postal savings system, with assets of over $300 billion, is still largely prohibited from investing abroad.

Insurance companies are much more constrained than pension funds in the United States (section 4). Even though the constraints are not now binding, they should be liberalized. There is no conceivable prudential need to limit foreign assets to 1 percent of the portfolio. Other countries also tend to take a somewhat restrictive attitude toward foreign investment by insurance companies, or at least toward investment in developing countries. In Britain, the Department of Trade should investigate and presumably approve a number of developing-country stock exchanges—starting with Amman, Bangkok, and Seoul—so that investments held on those markets will qualify for investment-linked policies (section 4).

As far as the bond markets are concerned, most of the smaller industrial countries continue to regulate the issue of foreign bonds by a queuing system. Those countries that operate such a system could usefully give preference to issues by developing countries.

It is not suggested that any of the above constraints are individually onerous or that the removal of all of them would have any dramatic impact. Their liberalization would remove a potential obstacle to flows of the size and form that we have called for and would indicate the assent of the industrial countries to a program of stimulating more risk-oriented investment. But, to have any major impact on the magnitude of flows, it would almost certainly be necessary to go beyond liberalization and provide preferential treatment for developing-country borrowers (as suggested above in respect to bond issues).

The case for seeking preferential treatment seems particularly strong in the case of the world's current major surplus country, Japan. Some observers have argued that prolonged maintenance of such a large current account surplus represents an abnegation of international responsibility. The standard reply is that making savings available to the rest of the world ought to provide benefits rather than costs to other countries. In principle this should be true: the problem is that at the moment those savings are almost all being placed in the United States, thus magnifying the overvaluation of the dollar, reducing income and hence savings in the United States, and building up massive distortions whose future unwinding is likely to be exceedingly costly. Practice would be brought more in line with principle if this problem were resolved by guidelines that called on Japanese institutional investors to hold at least (say) 25 percent of their foreign portfolios in the form of investments in developing countries. Such guidelines should be effective in view of the close relations between the Japanese government and the major financial institutions.

One other initiative could constructively be taken by the governments of some industrial countries. It is one where the natural candidates are some of the smaller countries with important primary product exports, like the Scandinavians (or perhaps Australia or Canada). It was argued in section 4 that there would be major advantage to many developing countries in being able to borrow by issuing commodity-linked bonds, but that this is at present impractical because there is no market for such bonds and only borrowers with the "best names" command sufficient confidence to be able to pioneer the introduction of a new asset. Chile or Zambia cannot pioneer the issue of copper-linked bonds—but Finland or Sweden could pioneer the introduction of pulp-linked bonds. Once such a market was successfully established, developing countries could start issuing commodity-linked bonds. In making this possible, it is conceivable and even likely that the industrial country that chose to pioneer would do itself a favor as well.

Private Investors

Another recent study by the Institute for International Economics (Bergsten, Cline, and Williamson 1985) has addressed the question of possible modifications in the form of commercial bank lending to developing countries. The main recommendations made in that study were directed to the banks, and may be summarized as follows.

- The banks should be willing to negotiate "Mexico-style packages," involving reduced charges, multiyear rescheduling, and longer maturities, with any debtor country that requests such a package and that has implemented a serious adjustment program that shows promise of succeeding.

- The banks should in future voluntarily offer variable maturity loans and/ or loans with RIACs to their developing-country clients, in return for a somewhat higher spread, in order to lessen the risks of interest-rate variations that fall on the borrowers under current arrangements.

- In the event of a renewed deterioration in the external environment confronting the developing countries (as a result, for example, of a new recession or a surge in interest rates), the banks should again cooperate with the IMF in assembling sufficient "involuntary lending" to sustain countries through the crisis.

One further issue relevant to the banks has emerged from the current study. Until now the banks have been the leading opponents of proposals to subordinate general obligation credits by creating new preferred creditors. As indicated in section 4, we sympathize with the principle but judge that it is taken too far when it is used to prevent the escrowing of export proceeds that might permit quasi-equity or stand-alone finance where the lender accepts the commercial risks. We therefore urge the banks to modify their stance on the general issue in this limited circumstance.

The main emphasis in the present study has been on the need to bring new actors, who are in a better position to share the inherent risks because of their greater scope for diversification as well as their special knowledge of particular commercial risks, into the business of lending to developing countries. These actors include corporations with direct, operational links to projects in developing countries as well as portfolio investors—primarily mutual funds, pension funds, and insurance companies, but also (for example) endowment managers and individuals. Such investors are unlikely to start buying the liabilities of developing countries as a matter of philanthropy. Indeed, they have a duty to their shareholders or clients to make the best possible investments, in terms of the hard-headed criteria of expected return, risk, and liquidity. This happens to require them not to overlook opportunities to make attractive investments in developing countries out of ignorance, prejudice, conservatism, or inertia.

Apart from direct investment, investment by nonfinancial corporations is most likely in quasi-equities and conceivably commodity price-linked instruments. Quasi-equities such as revenue-sharing contracts could significantly expand the scope for those actors with special expertise regarding relevant commercial risks, but who are at a disadvantage with regard to noncommercial (transfer) risks that are overlaid on commercial risks in direct investment. Commodity-linked securities could provide corporations with increased hedging opportunities.

The success of both types of instruments in large part depends on increasing the scope for unbundling commercial and noncommercial (transfer) risks. The private sector could contribute significantly to this through the expansion of country-risk insurance, which up to now exists on a relatively small scale.

Development of a market for country-risk insurance would presumably help to sustain the flow of commercial bank lending to developing countries and ease the problem of overconcentration of developing-country risk on the commercial banks. (See Bergsten, Cline, and Williamson 1985, pp. 110–

115, for a full analysis.) It would also increase the attractiveness of lending or investment entailing commercial risks to firms or lenders with the requisite expertise but reluctant to take large noncommercial transfer risks. Ironically, one group of investors that might derive great benefit from the existence of such insurance is local citizens who by virtue of their knowledge of local conditions have a comparative advantage in taking particular commercial risks but who also want to reduce their inherently large country-risk exposure.

As far as portfolio investors are concerned, it has been argued above that some investment opportunities in some countries already offer an attractive combination of expected return, risk, and liquidity. Many more such opportunities would be created if the developing countries modify their policies as called for above, and if the multilateral institutions adopt the suggestions made below. Nonbank asset managers in developed countries have a responsibility to their clients, which happens to coincide with the interests of the developing countries, to consider such assets on their merits, and to undertake the hard research that may indeed be needed to satisfy themselves (and in the process satisfy their fiduciary responsibilities) that those merits do indeed justify the commitment of funds.

Multilateral Institutions

The longer-term vision of financial intermediation to the developing countries that we have explored in the preceding pages is one that would involve a much greater role for the private sector—because it is the private sector that is accustomed to questioning whether prospective returns justify risk taking, and risky investments are the necessary counterpart to risk shifting by the borrowers. But we also believe that the MDBs have a vital role to play both in fostering the development of the instruments needed for the expansion of private investment and in sustaining an adequate level of capital flows in the interim until private investment can build up.

During the 40 years since it was founded, the World Bank introduced major operational programs in a series of areas as these have been identified as development priorities—infrastructure, agriculture, rural development, structural adjustment, Africa. In contrast, its only major initiatives to increase the scope for liability management by developing countries have been the cofinancing program and the MIGA proposal. In 1985, however, the Bank broadened its vision by choosing to make debt management the subject of the *World Development Report*. This initiative should be followed up by a decision to make debt management, both the restructuring of existing liabilities and new borrowing, a major operational focus for country programs in the next decade. The quality of the comments received on the manuscript of this study from several members of the World Bank staff was such as to allay any concerns that the Bank might lack the human resources to rise to this challenge.

If that is done, then the Bank will become intimately involved in helping developing countries choose appropriately among the array of possible approaches that have been explored above. The most appropriate techniques will differ from one country to another, and perhaps also from one decade to another. Naturally one would hope and expect that this would lead the Bank to ask itself whether it is currently providing loans on terms best suited to the needs of its members, or whether it should not (for example) be considering offering interest-rate caps (at a cost determined by its own cost of covering by buying options) or loans based on the constant-real-payment formula (section 4).

In addition to proffering advice and modifying its own lending terms, we have indicated in this study how the Bank (and other MDBs) could play a strategic role in unbundling risks and thus facilitating risk shifting. In particular, we have called on the MDBs to accept a role in monitoring the implementation of pricing rules and providing guarantees against transfer risk, so as to support the introduction of quasi-equity and stand-alone finance.

The IFC has the authority to invest directly in quasi-equity (or equity) instruments in the private sector and has just had its capital doubled to enable it to expand its activities. But the IFC is still too small and is precluded from providing finance to the public sector, which is the World Bank's preserve, except in special circumstances (as when a public enterprise is capable of standing alone and is due to be divested). For better or worse, most developing countries have extensive public sectors, which often embrace productive and export-oriented enterprises. Unfortunately the World Bank's Articles preclude its own extension of quasi-equity finance to such companies, and indeed require the Bank to make only general obligation loans guaranteed by the government of the borrowing country. The Bank has therefore not been involved in the design of risk-sharing investments. Even without a change in its Articles, however, the Bank could take the lead in designing quasi-equity instruments which it could cofinance with corporate or institutional investors.

The IFC has already been active in promoting the establishment of investment funds to undertake equity investment in emerging markets. This is an initiative that should be fully supported, especially by the potential host countries.

As noted, one area in which we would support a further direct injection of public money would be to provide the nucleus of a guarantee fund to back a collective of developing countries in the issue of long-term index-linked bonds (section 4). The initial scale could appropriately be modest: a pilot scheme would be sufficient to test the conjecture that money provided in the form of guarantees to such a scheme would have a high leverage in terms of the size of the loans that it could induce. The best chance of launching such a scheme may arise on a regional rather than a global basis. If, for example, the United States in particular or the West in general were to seek an appropriate response to Henry Kissinger's (1985) call for a Marshall Plan for Latin America, a plausible vehicle would be to endow the Inter-American Development Bank with a meaningful-sized guarantee fund, thus enabling it to sponsor the type of scheme outlined. Or if Japan were to conclude that the duties of a surplus country demand more than it has done so far, it might consider taking the lead in endowing the Asian Development Bank with such a guarantee fund. The funds that might be attracted by such an initiative could turn out to be large, although our table 9 has allowed only for $1 billion to $2 billion a year from this source. If it did turn out that substantial funds were available, the instrument could provide a mechanism for funding outstanding bank debt.

While our primary focus has been on charting the course for financial intermediation beyond the debt crisis, we recognize that there will be a difficult transitional period until borrowers again achieve normal market access. During this period the MDBs can play a particularly useful role in facilitating financial restructuring.

Under current circumstances, stand-alone financing in exchange for general obligation financing would require the agreement of general creditors. This is because it would create senior claims on certain export revenues, thus subordinating the claims on these flows of existing creditors. Existing lending agreements typically include negative pledge clauses that rule out such subordination without the lenders' consent. To persuade them to give this consent, general creditors would require some offsetting benefit.

In the case of new projects, this benefit could be in the form of new covenants assuring that the projects would not divert existing foreign-exchange proceeds. Such covenants might be monitored by existing multilateral agencies such as the IMF or the Bank for International Settlements (BIS) or by cooperative financial institutions such as the Institute of International Finance, whose membership is comprised of commercial banks involved in international lending, or the Japan Center for International Finance, a similar institution that recently has begun to rate developing-country credit.

Given the complexity of the required arrangements, it is most likely that such an exchange would take place as part of a refinancing package involving commercial lenders, the IMF, and the World Bank. In such a package, the World Bank, for example, might extend a structural adjustment loan where one of the policy targets would be the restructuring of existing liabilities and, through guarantees or colending, catalyze the flow of some net new lending. These might be stand-alone claims and could be B-loans under the Bank's cofinancing program: such claims might be taken up by existing lenders in place of some of their general claims, or by new nonbank institutional lenders. The benefit to existing creditors of such an arrangement, notwithstanding its creation of new senior claims, would be the partial repayment of their existing general claims coupled with an improvement in the quality of their remaining claims through the injection of new loans, the immediate reduction or stretch-out of debt service on the stand-alone portion of the package, and the creation of a sounder, more disciplined financial structure for the country.

We turn now to the shorter run question, of how the international institutions can help maintain an adequate flow of finance to the developing countries over the next few years. We have three proposals regarding the MDBs, but choose first to mention a natural and important role for the IMF.

Table 4 indicates that we have projected reserve accumulation of $11 billion by the indebted developing countries in 1987, but that according to present intentions there is unlikely to be an SDR allocation. A simple way of helping the developing countries to achieve the desirable addition to their capital inflow would be to use the SDR system for the purpose for which it was invented, namely to permit nonreserve centers to build up their reserves without the need to run payments surpluses. One of the present authors has argued the case for an SDR allocation at length (Williamson 1984), and concluded that there was a good case for annual allocations of at least $9 billion. Some 30 percent of such an allocation, or almost $3 billion, would accrue to the indebted developing countries. Accordingly, we have included such a sum in table 9. Note that this would still require the developing countries to earn or borrow the bulk of their reserve increases (doubtless extending credit to the US Treasury when they buy their reserves).

Our first proposal for MDB action to alleviate the foreign-exchange stringency of the developing countries concerns the World Bank's disbursement procedures. At present the Bank has a very substantial pool of liquid assets, which has recently been of the order of $17 billion. Doubtless the Bank needs a substantial buffer of liquid assets to permit continued disbursements to its clients and assure uninterrupted service of its debt if it becomes necessary, for whatever reason, to reduce the scope of its ongoing borrowing program for a time. Furthermore, the Bank manages its assets actively and has made a very creditable rate of return up to now. Nevertheless, the contrast between the comfortable liquidity position of the Bank and the desperate situation of many of its clients raises the question as to whether some portion of its liquid funds might not be put to even better use.

The Bank could stand willing to extend to more of its own operations the ingenious innovation that it recently introduced to resolve a similar complaint regarding disbursement of the cash raised by B-loans. Nowadays the B-loan is paid to the central bank of the country involved immediately after the loan has been agreed, and the central bank then undertakes gradual disbursement to the project (in line with disbursement of the World Bank's A-loan). There is no reason why under appropriate circumstances the World Bank should not similarly pay the A-loan directly to the central bank, or why it should not be prepared to extend this practice to its noncofinanced loans.[36] We suspect that such a step might be able to provide up to $2 billion a year of additional foreign-exchange receipts for several years without jeopardizing the Bank's liquidity or so shortening the disbursement pipeline as to threaten the leverage that it draws from this source.

This policy would doubtless need to be circumscribed in two important respects. First, the Bank should continue to monitor the disbursement of funds by the central bank to the project in its traditional, highly efficient way. Second, it should agree to accelerated disbursement only where it has confidence in the macroeconomic policies of the government and a broad set of policy understandings. A Fund program might be a factor giving the Bank confidence in the country's macroeconomic policies, but it ought not to be

---

36. This is indeed already done on a limited basis. The Bank typically places several months' anticipated expenditures in an account in the central bank which are then drawn down against receipts.

a precondition. (Colombia is a good example of a country without a Fund program that we would hope would benefit from such an initiative.)

A second area where the Bank could assist in the short term would be through expanding its present cofinancing program (as well as pursuing the innovations already discussed). The Bank indeed seems anxious to move forward in this area: the reluctance has come either from governments (in the case of the more creditworthy countries) or banks (for the less creditworthy countries), with countries near the borderline of market creditworthiness having been the main ones involved so far. But the provisional agreement with Chile announced in mid-1985 may mark a breakthrough in this respect, since Chile is far from returning to voluntary market borrowing. In this case the Bank's proposed use of its guarantee authority, to give a 50 percent guarantee on a $300 million commercial bank loan to a Bank-approved road project which had the longest maturities in a $1,085 million package, seems to have been the vital ingredient in persuading the banks to overcome their reluctance to participate in another concerted lending package. One fervently hopes that this will prove a precedent. We have not, however, added any separate sum for cofinancing in table 9, since we suspect that this effort will be necessary to ensure that the commercial banks reach their base level.

A third important topic concerns the provision of adequate resources to permit the MDBs to sustain net transfers at an appropriate level. It is important that low-income creditworthy countries like China and India not be forced (or tempted) into excessive reliance on general obligation bank credit as the Latin Americans were: one debt crisis is one too many. And it is important that the World Bank be able to step up its lending, including program lending (such as structural adjustment and sector lending), to ensure that the minimum desirable increase in capital flows to developing countries is indeed achieved.

Table 9 reveals that, without allowing anything for increased World Bank lending, the proposals already discussed could conceivably yield as much as $19 billion, but might easily yield less than $11 billion a year. (Remember that these flows are not necessarily entirely additional.) To ensure the ability to achieve an increase of $15 billion a year, the Bank would have to be given the financial ability to step up its lending by at least $4 billion a year. Extra lending of $4 billion for 10 years would require a capital increase approaching $40 billion, an increase of some 60 percent. This is the minimal general capital increase that needs to be approved at the 1985 Fund-Bank Annual Meetings in Seoul to convince the world that the critical problem of securing adequate financial intermediation beyond the debt crisis is indeed being treated seriously.

6   Conclusions

The analysis presented in this study provides scant reason for complacency regarding the outlook for capital flows to developing countries. Even if most debtor countries can dispense with further concerted lending packages by 1987, the outlook on present trends will be for a level of capital flows well below the ideal. Indeed, in real terms the developing countries are likely to remain in significant net surplus on current account, implying a substantial outward transfer of real resources. Moreover, on present trends there is little reason to anticipate any major shift in financing modes away from their past domination by general obligation, floating-rate credits. And if the global economic environment turns out to be less satisfactory than was assumed in the projections presented in section 2, concerted lending may well remain necessary and the international capital market is unlikely to play its potential role of enabling the developing countries to cushion the impact of declining exports.

It would be unrealistic to expect that this unsatisfactory state of affairs can be remedied overnight. Nevertheless, determined action by all the parties involved could lead to improvements that would enable international capital mobility to come closer to realizing its potential. Actions are needed both to stimulate the volume of flows in the short run and to change their structure in the longer run, in such a way as to enable the developing countries to shift many of the risks to which they have been exposed in the past on to their creditors. It stands to reason that the lenders will be prepared to accept such risks only if they are rewarded by the expectation of commensurately higher returns on those investments that prosper.

We have identified a number of financial instruments that could be exploited to promote a restructuring of international financial flows along these lines. The most promising candidates are:

- investment by nonbank financial institutions (mutual funds, pension funds, and insurance companies) in equities quoted on the stock exchanges of developing countries

- investment by multinationals in projects with a return determined by a "quasi-equity" contract, such as production sharing, revenue sharing, or profit sharing

- lending by banks or other financial institutions on a stand-alone basis for export-oriented projects whose earnings could be escrowed to provide debt service provided that the project prospered

- long-term, index-linked bonds issued by a consortium of developing countries with a partial guarantee provided by donors endowing a modest guarantee fund

- commodity-linked bonds with a yield tied by formula to the prices of major commodities, which would be issued by the exporters of those commodities

- use of the swap markets to secure debt-service streams denominated in a currency bundle that matches the currencies of price determination of exports

- use of the options markets to cap interest rates on floating-rate borrowing.

A number of other possible techniques were examined in passing, such as the use of the constant-present-value formula to calculate payments due on commercial bank credits, FRNs, and World Bank loans.

Drawing full advantage from international capital mobility will require more than the introduction or exploitation of new financial instruments. It will also require important changes in attitude, such as a determination on the part of the debtor countries to maintain in future a proper degree of financial discipline and resist the temptation to overexpand when financial constraints finally ease. These countries must also recognize that external finance is a complement to, rather than a substitute for, the mobilization of domestic savings. Finally, they must be willing to pay a realistic price for the risk shifting that financial markets are potentially capable of supplying.

Given such attitudes, a number of concrete actions need to be implemented to further the twin objectives of augmenting the volume of capital flows and improving their terms. Initiatives called for in the study include:

- a decision by the World Bank to make developing-country debt management, both the restructuring of existing liabilities and new borrowing, a major operational focus for country programs; and to offer its clients debt terms appropriate to their situation

- a general capital increase for the World Bank of the order of $40 billion

- acceleration of World Bank disbursements for countries with prudent macroeconomic policies

- early consideration of a further major capital increase for the IFC

- approval of MIGA

- acceptance by the MDBs of a role in monitoring pricing rules and providing guarantees against transfer risk so as to support quasi-equity and stand-alone finance

- extension of cofinancing programs to cover such assets

- the resumption of substantial SDR allocations

- endowment of a modest guarantee fund to permit one or more of the regional development banks to act as agent for a consortium of developing countries in partially guaranteeing long-term indexed-linked bonds

- introduction by Japan and perhaps other creditor countries of guidelines suggesting that at least 25 percent (say) of foreign institutional investments be in developing-country liabilities

- an agreement among the industrial countries to resume the supply of official export credit promptly after a country takes realistic adjustment measures

- a decision by one of the primary-product-exporting industrial countries to launch commodity-linked bonds to pioneer the development of markets for these assets

- a willingness by the commercial banks to permit the escrowing of export proceeds from a project where the lender takes commercial risks through acceptance of a quasi-equity or stand-alone claim

- relaxation of restraints imposed by developing countries on direct investment and foreign purchases of equities and real estate

- creation of mutual funds designed to facilitate the repatriation of flight capital.

References

Bailey, Norman A. 1983. "A Safety Net for Foreign Lending." *Business Week*, 10 January.

Bank for International Settlements. 1984. *The Maturity Distribution of International Bank Lending.* Basel, July.

Bergsten, C. Fred, William R. Cline, and John Williamson. 1985. Bank Lending to Developing Countries: The Policy Alternatives. POLICY ANALYSES IN INTERNATIONAL ECONOMICS 10. Washington: Institute for International Economics.

Bergsten, C. Fred, Thomas Horst, and Theodore H. Moran. 1978. *American Multinationals and American Interests.* Washington: Brookings Institution.

Blitzer, Charles R., Donald R. Lessard, and James L. Paddock. 1984. "Risk Considerations and the Choice of Contract Forms for Oil Exploration and Development." *Energy Journal*, January.

Bolin, William H., and Jorge Del Canto. 1983. "LDC Debt: Beyond Crisis Management." *Foreign Affairs*, vol. 61 (Summer).

Chenery, Hollis B., and Michael Bruno. 1962. "Development Alternatives in an Open Economy: The Case of Israel." *Economic Journal*, March.

Cline, William R. 1984. *International Debt: Systemic Risk and Policy Response.* Washington: Institute for International Economics.

De Larosière, Jacques. 1985. "Remarks before the Economic and Social Council of the United Nations in Geneva on July 5." *IMF Survey*, 15 July.

Dornbusch, Rudiger, and Stanley Fischer. 1984. "The World Debt Problem." Report prepared for UNDP/UNCTAD and the Group of 24. Cambridge, Mass.: Massachusetts Institute of Technology, July. Processed.

Eaton, Jonathan, and Mark Gersovitz. 1981a. "Debt with Potential Repudiation: Theoretical and Empirical Analysis." *Review of Economic Studies*, vol. 48.

———. 1981b. *Poor Country Borrowing in Private Financial Markets and the Repudiation Issue.* Studies in International Finance, no. 47. Princeton, NJ: International Finance Section, Department of Economics, Princeton University.

Ehrlich, Edna A. 1981. "International Diversification by United States Pension Funds." Federal Reserve Bank of New York *Quarterly Review*, August.

Enders, Thomas O., and Richard P. Mattione. 1984. *Latin America: The Crisis of Debt and Growth.* Washington: Brookings Institution.

Fishlow, Albert. 1984. "The Debt Crisis: Round Two Ahead?" In *Adjustment Crisis in the Third World.* Edited by Richard E. Feinberg and Valeriana Kallab. New Brunswick, NJ: Overseas Development Council and Transaction Books.

—————. 1985. "Lessons from the Past: Capital Markets during the Nineteenth Century and the Interwar Period." *International Organization,* Summer.

Group of Ten. 1985. "Communiqué of the Ministers and Governors of the Group of Ten." Tokyo, 21 June.

Group of Thirty. 1984. *Foreign Direct Investment 1973–87.* New York.

Guisinger, Steven, et al. 1985. *Investment Incentives and Performance Requirements.* New York: Praeger.

Guttentag, Jack, and Richard Herring. 1985. "Innovations to Stabilize Credit Flows to Developing Countries." Wharton School, University of Pennsylvania, Philadelphia, May. Processed.

House of Commons Select Committee on the Treasury and Civil Service. 1983. *International Monetary Arrangements: International Lending by Banks.* London: Her Majesty's Stationery Office.

Ibbotson, Roger, and Lawrence Siegel. 1983. "The World Market Wealth Portfolio." *Journal of Portfolio Management,* Winter.

Inter-American Development Bank. 1984. *External Debt and Development Prospects in Latin America: Background and Prospects.* Washington.

International Monetary Fund. 1985. *World Economic Outlook.* Washington.

Kissinger, Henry A. 1985. "Building a Bridge of Hope to Our Latin Neighbors," *Washington Post,* 25 June.

Lessard, Donald R. 1977. "Risk Efficient External Financing for Commodity Exporting Countries." *Cuadernos de Economía,* May.

—————. 1983. "North-South Finance: Implications for Multinational Banking." *Journal of Banking and Finance,* December.

Lessard, Donald R., and Phillip A. Wellons. 1979. *Financing Development: Innovations and Private Capital Markets.* Vienna: UNIDO, Joint Study on International Industrial Cooperation.

Lever, Lord Harold. 1983. "The International Debt Threat." *The Economist,* 30 April.

Marris, Stephen. 1985. *Deficits and the Dollar: The World Economy at Risk.* Washington: Institute for International Economics. Forthcoming.

McFadden, Daniel, Richard Eckhaus, Gershon Feder, Vassilis Hajivassilou, and Stephen O'Connell. 1985. "Is There Life after Debt? An Econometric Analysis of the Creditworthiness of Developing Countries." In *International Debt and the Developing Countries*. Edited by Gordon W. Smith and John T. Cuddington. Washington: World Bank.

McKinnon, Ronald I. 1964. "Foreign Exchange Constraints in Economic Development and Efficient Aid Allocation." *Economic Journal*, June.

Merton, Robert, and Scott Mason. 1984. "The Role of Contingent Claims Analysis in Corporate Finance." In *Recent Advances in Corporate Finance*. Edited by E. Altman and M. Subrahmanyan. New York: Irwin.

Modigliani, Franco, and Donald R. Lessard. 1975. *New Mortgage Designs for Stable Housing in an Inflationary Environment*. Boston: Federal Reserve Bank of Boston Conference Series, no. 14.

Moran, Theodore H. 1973. "Transnational Strategies of Protection and Defense by Multinational Corporations." *International Organization*, Spring.

Nowakowski, C.A. 1983. "Charting a Course for the Decade Ahead: Go Global or Go Aground." Stamford, Conn.: InterSec Research Corporation.

Oman, Charles. 1984. *New Forms of International Investment in Developing Countries*. Paris: Organization for Economic Cooperation and Development.

Stiglitz, Joseph E., and Andrew Weiss. 1981. "Credit Rationing in Markets with Imperfect Information." *American Economic Review*, June.

Van Agtmael, Antoine. 1984. *Emerging Securities Markets*. London: Euromoney Publications.

———. 1985. "New Scope for Investors in Emerging Securities Markets." *Euromoney Corporate Finance*, March.

Vernon, Raymond. 1971. *Sovereignty at Bay: The Multinational Spread of US Enterprises*. New York: Basic Books.

Williamson, John. 1977. "Transferência de Recursos e o Sistema Monetário Internacional." In *Estudos Sobre Desenvolvimento Econômico*. Rio de Janeiro: Banco Nacional do Desenvolvimento Econômico.

———. 1982. "The Why and How of Funding LDC Debt." In *Development Financing: A Framework for International Financial Cooperation*. Edited by S. Al-Shaikhly. Boulder, Col.: Westview Press.

———. 1983. *The Open Economy and the World Economy*. New York: Basic Books.

————. 1984. *A New SDR Allocation?* POLICY ANALYSES IN INTERNATIONAL ECONOMICS 7. Washington: Institute for International Economics.

————. 1985. *Inflation and Indexation: Argentina, Brazil, and Israel.* Washington: Institute for International Economics.

World Bank. 1985. *World Development Report.* Washington.

Other Publications from the Institute

POLICY ANALYSES IN INTERNATIONAL ECONOMICS SERIES

BOOKS

IMF Conditionality
John Williamson, ed./1983

Trade Policy in the 1980s
William R. Cline, ed./1983

Subsidies in International Trade
Gary Clyde Hufbauer and Joanna Shelton Erb/1984

International Debt: Systemic Risk and Policy Response
William R. Cline/1984

Economic Sanctions Reconsidered: History and Current Policy
Gary Clyde Hufbauer and Jeffrey J. Schott, assisted by Kimberly Ann Elliott/1985

SPECIAL REPORTS

1 **Promoting World Recovery: A Statement on Global Economic Strategy** *by Twenty-six Economists from Fourteen Countries/*December 1982

2 **Prospects for Adjustment in Argentina, Brazil, and Mexico: Responding to the Debt Crisis**
*John Williamson, ed./*June 1983

3 **Inflation and Indexation: Argentina, Brazil, and Israel**
*John Williamson, ed./*March 1985

118